MY MESS IS MY MESSAGE II

INSPIRING STORIES OF INCREDIBLE WOMEN WHO FOUND PURPOSE AND PROSPERITY THROUGH ADVERSITY

SOUL PURPOSE
PUBLISHING

Contents

FOREWORD

By Therese Skelly

In the pages of this beautifully written book, you will find stories from courageous women who understand that the challenges in their lives can serve a higher purpose. These women share resilience and courage and have claimed their inner power. Going through the transformation that their "mess" gave them, they were able to heal themselves from illness, grief, and broken relationships, and from this place they are now helping others. And while these are their individual stories, in truth, the stories are ours collectively.

At some point in your life, you will experience heartbreak. You will go through death, loss, betrayal, or other soul-crushing events that can bring you to your knees. Maybe you are there right now. If that's the case, I want you to know that there is hope!

I remember a few years ago when my beloved son was going through severe addiction and mental illness. Even though I have dealt with death and tons of trauma, seeing my son so lost and fearing for his life took me to my knees. I remember speaking to my minister and saying, "I'm pretty sure this will kill me because I cannot handle the stress." The truth is, I really didn't know how I could get through it. It was literally the hardest year I ever lived through. But here we are today. He's sober, using his "mess" to help others, and I'm strong, happy, healthy, and the best version of myself.

I'm here today, as are the authors, to let you know that you will get through whatever hardship you are dealing with! Life will become sweet again. You will find joy. Love will return. You can transform your life into something new and amazing. The author's and I have all been there and are sharing this book so you can find inspiration.

As you know, it's our stories that connect. Our stories are the thread of shared humanity that remind us that we are not alone. The stories serve to mark time, show growth, and provide a legacy. These stories were written with love. So much love.

To walk through the sometimes unspeakable pain or tragedy and emerge on the other side is the greatest accomplishment one can go through. You see, it would be easy to stay a victim or be stuck in anger. It would make sense to be bitter or have a hardened heart. It takes tremendous self-love to go through the experience, get the lessons from it, transmute the pain, and find the blessings. That's love. Loving ourselves enough to do the work our soul wants us to do and loving others enough to share our journey with them.

As you witness the beauty in each woman's story, may you feel the thread that connects us together. While the world works hard to divide, the stories serve to connect.

This is my wish for you. May the stories...

- Connect you more deeply to a strength that you may have forgotten.
- Remind you that you can overcome anything.
- Show you that there is always hope.
- Point the way to tools for healing and growth.
- Honor the journey of those who are willing to be the voice of truth.

It is my deepest joy to invite you to dive into "My Mess is My Message II."

Therese Skelly
The Intuitive Business Mentor
Website: www.ThereseSkelly.com
Facebook: https://www.facebook.com/therese.skelly

DINA MARAIS

Rewriting My Story

I grew up in scarcity, with a scarcity mindset of lack deeply ingrained in my being that took sixty-three years to fully transform. There have been periods of blissful abundance too in my married life, specifically referring to money. I have been abundantly blessed with a happy marriage of 40 years, a life partner who adored me, and three amazingly bright and beautiful children.

These periods of financial abundance were not due to me but to my husband. Although I did contribute to them greatly at times, it was mostly my husband who brought home the bacon. He could manage a budget of a billion dollars with ease and lead hundreds of people in his corporate career. He was a master of delegation and empowering people to own their genius. After his untimely death earlier this year, I had so many messages from people who worked with him and said that he was the best boss they ever worked for.

He took care of me, and I always felt safe with him. No matter what storms we faced, with him by my side, I was okay. Until he couldn't. I was on my own. Looking back at the unfolding of our life journeys, it is nothing short of awe-inspiring to see the hand of God guiding us toward Home.

My husband was a visionary; he had such a different outlook on life. It was as if he could see the bigger picture of the Universe. He knew what was best, but I never listened when his advice was not what I wanted to hear. I followed my own decisions, sometimes with disastrous financial results, but he never blamed me.

I remember when, in 2008, I had the idea of creating a Life Coaching Diary for 2009. On impulse, I printed a thousand copies at an astronomical cost but could only sell a few, all because it never crossed my mind to do some research first. If I had, I would have realised that all retailers place their orders for diaries nearly a year in advance. The other idea I had that also resulted in a huge financial loss was developing an online self-coaching system. It was brilliant in concept but not well thought through in terms of target market and adaptability to work on phones as well. Again, if I had done some research, I would have discovered that there were already platforms that I could have utilised and did not need to develop my own platform from scratch.

This has been my pattern: I get an amazing idea and leap into action. I have the ability to take a concept, see the big picture as well as the details immediately, and create it.

When I discovered NLP—Neuro-Linguistic Programming—I knew that I had found my purpose and that I never wanted to do anything other than coaching. With my IT background, it was as easy as breathing for me to design and develop coaching courses.

What was not easy was getting clients for my life-changing programs. At one stage, my daughter, a gifted marketer herself, reached out to help me. We devised a plan that seemed so easy on paper, requiring a few clients to have a successful program. Still, it didn't work. I got crickets for results. I couldn't understand it. I was doing all the right things. All the ideas I acted on felt so aligned with me that I could feel it in my heart; I could feel the YES in every fibre of my being! Yet, when I implemented them, nothing happened. It was so confusing and frustrating. I didn't even know how to pray anymore. It felt that whatever I was doing was wrong. I was missing something very important.

When I received the opportunity to start my own publishing company, I knew this was for me. But I didn't have the money to do the program. I had to let it go. Then the opportunity came past again, and I still knew this was what I wanted, but once again, I couldn't sign up. It came the third time, and I decided that there must be a way for me to do this. My husband gave me the money to get started.

From there, it flowed. I knew the title of my first book would be My Mess Is My Message, and I filled the book in three months. It was a thrilling experience, and I enjoyed every moment and every part of the process. I loved recruiting the co-authors and speaking to incredible women who said yes to me without knowing me. Learning the different aspects of publishing and finding my way while leading them to become international bestselling authors was so fulfilling. I was amazed at my natural talent for guiding the authors to write their best stories. My gratitude for the loving guidance I received from my mentor, Monique Alvarez, and her husband and business partner, Derek, knows no bounds. She is one of my Earth Angels. I believe she was sent to help me.

The project was completed successfully. My Mess Is My Message was an international bestseller in the US and Australia with 17 international bestselling authors. With this experience, I have broken through so many limitations—money, self-belief, self-worth, and confidence in my new publishing business.

I was ready for the next book and immediately decided on a title. Knowing the process, I created my information page and started to recruit co-authors. Quite quickly, I had a sale, and I thought this book was going to be filled in no time. But that didn't happen. Sales were painfully slow after the first one. There was no momentum. Self-doubt took over, and all I could see was letting people down and money drying up. I became even more despondent seeing other publishers rocking it, and thinking that the first book was just a fluke, that this was not for me, and that I was not good enough to attract the people I wanted for this book. It seemed that Success with Source was just too big a title for me to birth into the world.

It was such a long year with very little happening in my business. I didn't even think about doing coaching, as I was obsessed with the book. I felt so powerless, putting in so much effort with no return. It became a burden that I just wanted to escape from. But there was no escape; there were people who trusted me with their money and a promise to become an international bestselling author. There was no other way out but through. *But how?*

The year dragged on painfully slowly on getting sales and money in and frightfully fast to month ends. One bright light was our baby grandson, and we were delighted to watch his progress on Zoom. We had such a longing to see our children again and to hold our darling baby in our arms, but there was no way we could afford to visit them. Then my daughter and precious son-in-law, who live in Spain, invited us for two weeks over Christmas, all expenses paid. We could celebrate our grandson's first birthday. I was so excited, I couldn't wait.

What we didn't know was that my husband's health was deteriorating. The flights to Spain and back accelerated his illness, and shortly after we returned, he passed away in February. There were no assets, and there were no life policies providing me with a cushy sum of money. I was on my own. Fortunately, my children took care of the funeral arrangements, and my sons stayed with me for three months, supporting me financially and emotionally.

I realized that this was not the way I wanted to live—for my children to support me. My goodness! I was a talented woman. I had a business that had enormous potential, and it was time I figured out how to make it work! No more feeling like the victim. No more playing small. It has been more than a year; enough is enough. Something's got to give.

I made the decision that this book was getting filled now, and I set a date for it to be published. Making that decision was the best thing I did because suddenly the path to accomplishing this was revealed to me. What I found was that people are very reasonable and accommodating when we are being honest and transparent. I cancelled an agreement with a team to publish the book that would have required a sum of money I didn't have. I found another editor, and I bought the software to format the book myself. With my IT background, it was easy to figure out, and I enjoyed doing it, plus I felt more in control of the end product.

Once I had the production sorted, the only thing that was outstanding was filling the last few chapters. I decided to invite leaders in the field of vibrational alignment as guest writers. These were women that I admired and respected and that I felt would do the book justice. It was very important to me to make sure that the intention behind the book was met and that the promise of the subtitle, learn from women who practice vibrational alignment in their business, was fulfilled.

In the author meetings leading up to the launch, I felt so intimidated to be leading these powerful women to write their chapters and to be giving them feedback on what they wrote. But I knew that it was time for me to step into this identity of a leader or not be in this profession. It took all my courage to take the lead and direct the authors to what I needed from them. The feedback was amazing! One by one, they all said that they enjoyed working with me, that I was a powerful leader, and that they loved my energy.

It dawned on me that these women did not see me as small and insignificant. They respected me, and I commanded respect. They saw me as an equal. It was time to do that for myself. I realised that upgrading my identity and seeing myself as a successful publisher was crucial to the success of my business.

The launch arrived quickly. It was time to fulfill my promise to the co-authors that they would become international bestselling authors because the book would be an Amazon #1 Bestseller in more than one country. Running a bestselling launch can feel like a gamble, but actually it's a very calculated process. Still, there are many variables at play. I prayed and knew I had to trust and surrender to God.

I was not disappointed. Success with Source soared to number one in four countries in July! I was over the moon with joy and relief. And I was also filled with such gratitude that it felt like my heart was going to explode. I decided that I would never ever doubt God again and to trust and surrender to the power and love of God-in-me. Everyone was happy and partying! 19 International bestselling authors celebrated their status!

When Success with Source was stagnant, I thought to start another book to get my mind off what was not working and also to bring in money. I decided that the next title would be My Mess Is My Message II. Given that the first volume was such a success and easily filled, I thought this would be my saviour. I was wrong. Three months after I made the big announcement, I had a sale in January, then nothing, then another sale in May, then nothing.

It was following the same pattern as the previous book, Success with Source. I thought to myself that this was not the way to fill a book! At this rate, it's going to take years to publish a multi-author book. It was just not sustainable!

I knew I was the problem. I was not in vibrational alignment. I have always been fascinated by manifesting. How was it that some people appear as if they were born with the proverbial silver spoon in their mouth while others experience lifelong struggle? If it was all about vibrational alignment, what was the secret? What did the people who were manifesting with ease know that the rest of us didn't? I have been a fan and avid follower of Abraham Hicks, Dr. Joe Dispenza, and Bob Proctor, and I knew the theory of vibrational alignment inside out. What was I missing?

The answer I sought, was in the teachings of Marina Jacobi. She explained that we are creating two timelines simultaneously: a low or lower vibrational timeline of our current reality and a higher vibrational timeline of our desired reality. These two timelines merge after a while and create a third timeline that is the result of the reality we experienced the most. So, when we meditate and visualise what we desire and feel the elevated emotions, our frequency elevates into the high vibrational timeline, and when we get triggered into fear or doubt, our frequency drops into the low vibrational timeline.

That video was a lightbulb moment. I could see how I couldn't manifest my desired reality because I must have allowed my frequency to be pulled down into the lower reality more than I was aware of. The Universal Laws work in precise Divine Order. The results spoke for themselves. I knew I had to find a way to sustain that higher vibration frequency.

A friend mentioned how effective it was to grow one's audience by making a video every day. I remembered my mentor, Monique, saying the same thing. How she did a Facebook Live every day for a month and how she grew her audience and client base. That inspired me to make a daily video sharing my knowledge, just to express myself and to cultivate the habit of consistency. I didn't have a coaching program, as I had been focusing exclusively on publishing. Soul-aligned manifesting had been on the back burner for a while then. But I felt the need to talk about this. I sat down and immediately made a list of a hundred video titles.

What I realised was that by recording a video talking about the topics of self-mastery, soul-alignment, self-love, and vibrational alignment, I was integrating these truths into my being and I started to sustain that higher frequency.

What was even more amazing was that I did not decide to make the daily videos to get something; I created them because I enjoyed it. Manifesting is my passion. It was and still is huge fun for me, and it gave me profound satisfaction and gratification. The consistency paid off. My subscribers on YouTube have more than doubled, and the views have exploded compared to before. I have even received comments.

Then I received the idea of practicing gratitude. One of the co-authors of Success with Source mentioned how that made a huge difference in her life. At first, I thought, but I was doing that! I felt grateful all the time! The idea came back to me again, and I decided to buy the book The Magic by Rhonda Byrne and implement the practices prescribed. It intensified my love and compassion for myself and others.

Self-love is the ultimate gratitude to God for creating you. – Dina Marais

Magic started to unfold. Suddenly, people started to buy the chapters of My Mess Is My Message II. Authors seemed to come from out of nowhere. Nearly every author I had a conversation with joined the book. It felt as if I was on a magic carpet ride! It was just so magnificently beautiful! I was in awe. Where I had two sales in eight months, I now had seventeen sales in two months and ten days, and I gave away three chapters.

The real magic was that I knew what I had done that caused this turnaround, and it was replicable. I always knew and said that the brain learns by repetition. So often we want a quick fix, and so we jump from one thing to the next, and in doing that, nothing sticks. The subconscious mind never gets the message that things are changing. In other words, we don't change. And nothing changes until we change.

I have shifted something profoundly in myself. Besides shifting my vibration to a higher level permanently, I have also integrated a new identity of somebody who is successful and prosperous and aligned with my Divine Self.

I have rewritten my story to be in alignment with who I really am.

I became more curious. I wanted to see what my name and birth date meant in numerology. It was unreal! My numbers confirmed my natural talent for taking an idea and making it work on the material plane, which is what I am here to do. All the words derived from the numbers confirmed my personality. What is more, is that the number of my birth surname means to stand on my own two feet. My body shivered. I was at last at that place in my life for the first time, standing on my own two feet.

But that is not all. Last year, I discovered Human Design and was drawn to *Quantum Human Design™ created by Karen Curry Parker.* Just from that initial introduction and explanation of my chart, I immediately knew that I was not following the strategy for my type. Human Design is a combination of Eastern and Western Astrology, the Hindu Chakra System, the Chinese I'Ching, the Judaic Kabbalah, and quantum physics. In this system, there are five types, nine centres, 64 gates, 12 profiles, and 36 channels. Your chart reflects your design as determined by the planets at the time of your birth. Just like in astrology, your chart is determined by the time and place you were born. Your chart shows your type, strategy, and profile.

In Quantum Human Design™, I am a 3/5 Time Bender/Manifesting Generator, and looking at what it meant on a surface level, I saw that my strategy was to wait to respond. That sounded Greek to me. Wait, for what? Waiting for something to show up in my external world to confirm that I can go ahead and take action. I knew that I had never done that consciously. Every idea that I have ever had, I acted on immediately. I assumed that feeling the alignment within and my heart saying yes was my cue to jump into action. I assumed wrong.

No wonder I rarely experienced flow. No wonder so many people do not experience life to their full potential. So, when I saw this for the first time, I knew I had to know more.

Two things stood out in my history. I wasn't living my Quantum Human Design™. I definitely was not waiting before leaping into action, as I ought to do. The second was that I was not maintaining a high vibrational frequency consistently enough to create a higher vibrational timeline.

I had now learned how to sustain my vibrational frequency, but I was still not sure about how to wait, and what that would look like. And I definitely did not want to screw up this beautiful thing I had going with the Universe. I knew that this was a crucial piece to get right. Already, I had so many ideas, and I had to restrain myself from leaping into action. It's like I need a restraining order against my ego.

Then came the opportunity to study Quantum Human Design™, created by Karen Curry Parker, and get certified. (I responded to something external; Karen offered a challenge, and I joined.) I knew that this was the missing link for most people to manifest their dreams, as it was for me. I am now a Quantum Human Design™ Level 2 Specialist at the time of publishing this book, studying further to qualify as a Certified Quantum Human Design™ Transformation Coach.

In hindsight, I can see how I followed my Quantum Human Design™ by becoming a publisher. And I can see where I didn't follow it. What's more, my Quantum Human Design™ correlates with the numbers that I tested with numerology. This self-awareness is priceless. I am in awe of the Divine Purpose of every one of us!

I sincerely believe that knowing my Quantum Human Design™ and the story of who I really am, rewriting my human story to be in alignment with my soul, and knowing how to sustain the energy frequency of my desired reality, especially while waiting to respond, are essential to manifesting my dreams.

I feel called to share this with entrepreneurs so that we can all accelerate manifesting our dreams to the benefit of humanity. That's why we are here, right? Being equipped to fulfill our soul contracts with ease and without being crippled by our human stories.

ABOUT THE AUTHOR

Dina Marais is the founder of Soul Purpose Publishing and Coaching, a 4-time international bestselling author, Soul-Aligned Manifesting Coach, and artist.

She works with established entrepreneurs to unleash the potential of their brands, elevate their visibility, and skyrocket their credibility by becoming bestselling published authors. She publishes solo and multi-author books.

She is continuously co-creating inspirational multi-author books to give entrepreneurs a voice and share their powerful stories to uplift humanity, so feel free to see if the latest title resonates with you.

Dina has been involved in transformation coaching since 2002. Her expertise is grounded in NLP-Neuro-Linguistic Programming, Neuro-Semantics, PNI-PsychoNeuroImmunology, and quantum physics.

She is a Certified Quantum Human Design™ Level 2 Specialist, on her way to qualifying as a Certified Quantum Human Design™ Transformation Coach, created by Karen Curry Parker.

As a Soul-Aligned Manifesting Coach, Dina empowers entrepreneurs to embody their true Self and manifest their highest goals and desires by rewriting their human stories, living their Quantum Human Design™, and integrating a higher energy vibrational frequency.

Website: https://dinamarais.com

Facebook: https://www.facebook.com/dinamarais1/

Instagram: https://www.instagram.com/coachdinamarais/

YouTube: https://www.youtube.com/@dinamarais

Email: dina@dinamarais.com

DR. KATIE FIELDS

Shadow Me

My story is called Shadow Me, first and foremost because I am writing about my Shadow– the aspects of me I have kept hidden and stowed away for many years. This story is also an invitation for you to join me in discovering and uncovering your Shadow. Doing Shadow work is a deep, uncomfortable journey of reuniting and liberating the parts of ourselves we have disowned and abandoned–those parts of us we keep locked away in our subconscious in fear they will destroy us and life as we know it. Our Shadow has its origins in our childhood, when we learned it wasn't safe to be our real selves, when we had little power to stand up to others and speak our truth, and when we had to adapt to feel safe and secure. This story is an act of me reconciling and embracing my Shadow, because only then can I truly begin to feel whole, secure, and at ease in the world.

It's not easy to meet our Shadow, and yet it shows up relatively regularly in our day to day lives. My Mess is the direct result of denying my Shadow. Whether I acknowledge it or not, it's been following me for decades, haunting and sabotaging my life along the way. While it may seem like I've done pretty well from the outside, it's been through a facade, a thin, protective layer of myself that reflected whatever I perceived others wanted from me. The real me has been covered, hidden away since I was little, frightened away by an environment that consistently communicated that who I was wasn't good enough.

My story isn't unique. In fact, I feel like it's quite ordinary. The experiences I had that created my Shadow are common and not extreme. That is one of the reasons I wanted to share it. I hope you will see yourself in aspects of my story and realize you too have a Shadow; we all do. You don't have to go through something horrific. I hope that you will feel permission to see yourself as worthy of having darkness without having been abused, neglected, or having witnessed something awful or terrifying. I also want to be clear that we don't have to blame or shame anyone for our darkness. As I understand it, it is a normal part of human development. It is a process of being covered and then noticing and committing to uncovering and reclaiming ourselves. Through this process, we learn to love ourselves– all of ourselves– more deeply and completely than we could have ever before.

It's hard to know where to begin my story. It's probably going to feel like I'm jumping around a bit. The most intense part would be when I said yes to writing this chapter. I was in a place of gut-wrenching heartache, having learned that my partner had cheated on me...again. It was compoundingly painful because I had fooled myself into believing things had changed. I felt like I betrayed myself and had kept myself in a dangerous situation. I wanted to run, but I also wanted to hide, something that I had done for years, yet I knew it hadn't served me very well. Hiding meant keeping what was happening to myself and not telling anyone, not even my closest friends or family. Hiding is something I am really good at, pretending everything is okay when it's not. That's how I feed my Shadow, with secrets steeped in shame.

Clearly, publishing this story is no way to hide. In fact, it's the opposite. I'm literally putting my story on display for the whole world–whoever wants to read it can. That is how we meet and befriend our Shadow. We do the opposite–the thing that makes us feel vulnerable. As you read this, I face my Shadow again and again. Choosing not to hide is healing. You reading this helps me heal. Thank you.

Writing this is scary. My partner was scared. I can't tell my story without incriminating him. Infidelity is not something people openly talk about, let alone write about in a published book. We also don't usually admit to staying in a relationship where we've been cheated on. But I'm here to break free of this harmful way of doing things. I would be betraying myself if I continued to hide. I'd stay in my mess. We kept it hidden for years. Telling my dad and a close friend were the scariest and most relieving experiences I've had through all of this. Surprisingly, telling them brought our relationships closer together. I feel more secure with both of them than I ever have before. Vulnerability with safe people can have a powerful impact on a relationship.

For me, leaving my partner would have actually been easier than staying. It would have been an escape. I could let go of a mess and start anew, like leaving a house full of hoarded clutter. I fantasized about being alone and not having to risk being hurt ever again. I didn't leave; I chose to stay, and this time I chose to look my darkness in the eye and sit down with it. I was tired of running. I surrendered, and then the magic began to happen.

Since this last betrayal, my partner has finally shown up for me in all the ways I've needed for so long. Really, for the first time in a relationship, I'm allowing myself to be taken care of. I finally feel like I am worthy of it and not a burden for wanting it. Given what he'd put me through, I felt like I finally deserved to have needs and was allowed to take up space, and I don't know that I would have arrived here without this happening to me. This is how our Shadow finds us. It looms over our lives, sending us invitation after invitation, until we finally accept and do the work. It's been right there waiting for me. If I wasn't ready now, it would show up again in some other way in the future, forever giving me the opportunity to return to myself.

This is probably a good place to mention that I am a couple's therapist who specializes in helping couples heal from infidelity. Before I embraced my Shadow, knowing my partner had been unfaithful to me several times was humiliating. It made me feel like a fraud. I was hiding behind a facade that presented me as someone who had it all figured out, like a home organizer whose house was a disheveled mess. Looking back, helping them was preparing me to do my own work. It built my confidence and was a surrogate for my healing. I am so grateful to those couples for helping me develop the courage to face my own mess in my own time.

They say therapists are wounded healers and that our specialties reveal something about our story. It's true. I am now willing and ready to own it. I want you to know that I don't have it all figured out. What I do know is that we all have a Shadow that lurks behind us, wanting our attention. Avoiding it makes it grow bigger, more intense. It sounds counterproductive, but looking at it and being with it can actually bring us peace. I am here to share the peace I have found and how I found it.

Staying with a partner who has hurt you is an incredibly difficult and personal decision. There is no rule for when to stay or when to leave. What I know about my relationship is that if I had left, I would have missed out on the opportunity to be true to myself and be loved and cared for by someone I love and care for, something I had never experienced. It feels strange to allow the one who has hurt me to care for me, but it has also provided deep healing. This is why I help couples. Our long-term partnerships can be incredibly healing, especially for our childhood wounds. They can also help us embrace our Shadow. Aside from our parents, our partners are our most meaningful attachment figures.

As a therapist, I have deep compassion for my clients and their decisions. I trust clients to know what is best for themselves, even if it takes time to discover it. I do my best not to impose my values or judgments on them and their lives. After all, they are the ones who have to live with themselves and their choices. But when it came to myself, I had trouble separating from the "shoulds" and the expectations I perceived from others. I felt like I had to end it. That saying, "Fool me once, shame on you, fool me twice, shame on me, fool me three times, and I'm an idiot," kept ringing through my mind.

I kept checking in with myself, seeing how I truly felt. After the initial shock, I did not feel like I wanted to leave. When I asked myself why, I answered, "Because he is my person." I didn't want anyone else. I couldn't see myself with anyone else. I just wanted him to stop hurting me.

A few weeks after I learned about this last betrayal, I went to an Energy Psychology conference. I attended a demonstration of the Emotional Freedom Technique (EFT) provided by the Association for Comprehensive Energy Psychology's Executive Director, Robert Schwarz. When I entered the room, I was not aware that I was going to volunteer to be the demo, but when it became apparent that the invitation was there, I said yes! - a further release of my Shadow. In front of a room full of people, Bob led me through my feelings about the recent betrayal. I started the demonstration in confusion and numbness from the pain and ended in a place of clarity and assurance of my path.

The experience reconnected me to my 5-year-old self, shut out by her older brother, who had been tasked with watching her while their parents worked. She was alone and lying on the floor outside his closed bedroom door. In the demonstration, I sat with her, tapped with her, and let her know I was with her now. She held my hand, and I took her to my current home and let her see the bedroom of my two little girls. She was excited to meet them and play. Bob and the EFT process helped me get to the underlying belief that it's not safe for me to let others take care of me. I was afraid I wouldn't know who I was if others took care of me. This belief originated from my childhood experience with my brother.

If my brother allowed me into his room, I had to do whatever he wanted, which meant I had to play video games I was too young to understand and then be criticized for not doing it right, or I'd have to listen to loud heavy metal music that hurt my ears, and I could only speak if I was spoken to. I wasn't allowed to be myself in his room. If I wanted to be minimally cared for and not alone, I had to do what he wanted, be his entertainment. Looking back, I was an outlet for his developing Shadow. He was 11, and my 5-year-old self was a burden to him.

It wasn't his fault; I'm sure he had no choice in the matter. He could tolerate me only if I did what served him.

In the demonstration, I could clearly remember the moment I "broke", kicking and screaming outside of his door, begging him to let me in so that I wasn't alone. I agreed to do whatever he wanted me to, even to keep his secret of sneaking out and going to his friend's house, which was breaking Mom and Dad's rules. Luckily, when he did go, he took me along, and I wasn't left at home alone. But wherever we went, I had to stay silent and essentially not be there. I learned to make myself small. I wasn't allowed to take up any space; I had to be a Shadow. What I wanted or needed didn't matter; I didn't matter. My Shadow grew, holding all of my wants and needs, shrouded in the shame of wanting and needing.

My once confident and connected self grew anxious and shy; I didn't want to ask anyone for anything. My needs were a burden. The only thing I needed was to be easy so others would be willing to be around me. I was the least needy kid, and, to enhance my easiness, I became an excellent people pleaser. I became an achiever; I made people proud to know me and want to be with me. My personality screamed, "Look how accomplished and wonderful I am, and as a great bonus, I'm not at all needy!"

I was driven to meet my own needs to protect myself from the rejection of others not wanting to care for me. I worked multiple jobs. Money was my safety net; it was how I would never need a favor from anyone ever again. It was the way I could endure my Shadow– the belief that I was a burden. If I did need something from someone, I could pay them to compensate them for their efforts spent on me. Relationships became completely transactional. I paid close attention and kept a mental accounting of what was "owed" to others.

I hated my neediness and regularly neglected many of my own needs. I ate poorly, had no downtime, and was annoyed that my minimal personal hygiene took so long. The only way I invested in myself was if it increased my ability to achieve and make money. I was running from my Shadow.

When I became a mother, my needs became incredibly difficult to hide from. Why did I have to spend 2 whole minutes twice a day brushing my teeth every single day?! Why did I have to pee and eat?! My anger spilled over to my girls when they had extended moments of neediness. Being sick or going through a growth spurt was incredibly annoying. Luckily for them, they were healthy, and their leaps were developmentally appropriate. I don't know what would have happened if I had had a special needs child. I felt incredibly guilty being a therapist and yelling at my children for their normal neediness. I knew they were small and depended on me. I beat myself up internally. I felt worse and worse about myself. I never asked for help. As far as I was concerned, I asked to get pregnant, and these kiddos were my burden to bear. What I now know is that I was being triggered; my Shadow was begging for attention.

This brings me to name the other population I love working with as a therapist: parents. If we let them, our children can be incredible teachers and healers for us. Becoming a parent has the potential to break generational patterns and free us and our children from harmful ways of being. What I've shared shows how the cycle could continue into the next generation. My Shadow of feeling like a burden was starting to make me see my children as burdens. Their needs made me feel unsafe because they led to me having needs, which ran the risk of me having to ask for help. If I continued ignoring my Shadow, I would have put their neediness into their Shadow, and they could potentially carry forward that burden.

Back to my relationship with my partner and the healing that occurred in the demonstration. I have never let a partner take care of me. Instead, I did all the doing and then built resentment, which inevitably poisons the relationship. Friends and family have pointed it out to me before, but I have never been willing to change. It never felt safe enough to ask for my needs to be met in a relationship; I just met their needs and hoped they would reciprocate. Since the most recent betrayal, my partner has taken on more of his share of parenting and has cared for me. I am no longer always the primary or default parent. I finally have permission to have needs and the opportunity to meet them.

My partner took on the complete care of the girls while I went to the energy conference. It was unlike any trip I've ever taken since we've been together. I felt no resentment from him; he seemed happy to have the opportunity to be the primary parent. I've always noticed how much he loved being the hero. He enlisted in the army, and he gives homeless people money and rides to hitchhikers. When our first daughter broke her arm at age 2, he did the incredibly hard task of holding her still to be x-rayed and then to have her cast cut off and reapplied–both terrifying experiences for a little person and the parent holding them still. When my beloved dog ran away, he dropped everything to help me find him. He is a good person. His neglected Shadow was driving his behavior.

My partner loves protecting and saving others and, I would rarely let him do that for me or the girls. My doing everything out of fear of being a burden left very little room for him to contribute. It appeared that I didn't need him in any way. If the girls were sick, I'd take off work. If they needed something, I would buy it. In the EFT demonstration, Bob helped me see how the flow of energy between us was blocked by my belief that I was a burden. He sensed that my partner was the kind of guy that needed to be needed. He said, "[Some] men want to slay the dragon and get the girl". That statement made me realize how much I had gotten in my own way. I noticed how the women my partner cheated on me with and, as far as I had been told, the women he had dated before me, had all been damsels in distress. I too was a damsel in distress in a sense when he met me. I was ending a marriage and my mom had just died. Interestingly and synchronously, the day of the demonstration with Bob was the 10th anniversary of my mom's passing. I am forever grateful for Bob and his warmth, sincerity, and love in that demo. I let Bob care for me, and it was so nourishing. The experience still brings tears to my eyes.

When I don't give others the opportunity to help and care for me, I limit my connection with them. I essentially eliminate the option by not expressing my needs and inviting them in. I now know this is a way we experience love. I have been severely limiting my love for myself, so much so that it led to betrayal, pain, and suffering. In being neglected, I began to neglect myself. This is how hurt people hurt others. I am so grateful I have the opportunity to see this and interrupt the cycle of harm.

I cannot be sure my partner will not cheat again; that is his journey. What I can do is allow my needs to be present and attended to. I will take care of myself, and I will let others care for me. I will notice the source of my impatience with my girls and ask for help. I will make it clear that they have full permission to have needs and be cared for. This is what is mine to do. This is how I will honor the messages from my mess and be with my Shadow.

As I continue my relationship with my partner, little me still watches for his dissatisfaction in caring for me. When I notice her doing that, I look at her and remind her that she has me. I'm here, and her needs are okay with me. If my partner ever decides he no longer wants to take care of me, including being faithful to me, I'll care for me and I'll be faithful to me. I am my primary source of love and care, and I'm deserving of love and care from others.

Loving my partner has been an incredible lesson, an invitation into my deepest darkness and into my highest Self. I choose love over fear. Choosing fear means running, hiding, barricading myself from hurt, and also from growth and becoming. Truly loving myself first allows me to be truly loved by another. These are the lessons I am learning.

ABOUT THE AUTHOR

Katie Fields is a woman on a journey to know and be her true, authentic self. She is unlearning the ways she had to be to survive her early experiences. Her path has inspired her to help others do the same.

Professionally, Katie is a therapist who practices through a transcendental psychodynamic lens. She is also an energy healer who offers Reiki, the Emotional Freedom Technique (EFT), and a variety of readings from tarot and oracle cards, the Akashic Records, and Human Design.

As an entrepreneur, Katie is developing CounSouling, an approach to healing and personal development through the reunion of Ego and Soul. She sees our human experience as a hero's journey where Ego leaves home (Soul) to venture into the world, experience life, and return home enlightened. CounSouling provides resources, guidance, and support for this transcendental journey.

At home, Katie enjoys spending time with her partner, their two daughters, and their pets. She appreciates how her family brings out the parts of her that need healing. As she returns to her true nature and her Ego reunites with her Soul, she plans to do more traveling, be more creative, and be present with herself and her loved ones.

Dr. Katie Fields, LMFT, LMHC

Website: https://fear-lesstherapy.com

Website: https://fearlesscounsouling.com

TRACEY A CHAPMAN

One Moment In Time: A World Changed

"*Pain is not a place to live; lighting our soul up and living is!*" ~ Tracey A Chapman

Embracing resilience.....

Growing up as a farmer's daughter, I played an active role in supporting my family on the farm. My father always emphasised the importance of giving our very best. If something didn't work out initially, he taught me to keep trying until I succeeded. This valuable lesson instilled a tremendous resilience that has carried me through life's challenges.

I grew up in Boyup Brook, a small town located in the southern region of Western Australia. Like many others in rural areas, I followed the traditional path of marrying at a young age, being only 21 at the time.

Following our marriage, my partner and I made the exciting decision to relocate from Boyup Brook to Collie to pursue our entrepreneurial ambitions. It was a thrilling new chapter for us, which became even more fulfilling when we were blessed with the arrival of our first child, Shannon. Just 20 months later, we were overjoyed once again as we welcomed our second child into the world, Tristan.

Oh, my goodness! Prepare to be amazed by these two absolutely adorable little boys, who could easily be mistaken for angels themselves! With their curly blond hair and precious cherub noses, they are the epitome of cuteness. And let's not forget those mesmerising eyes - Shannon with his enchanting brown eyes and Tristan with his captivating blue/grey eyes that seem to change with the light.

Right from the start, I had a crystal-clear vision of my life's aspirations. I firmly believed that the power to shape my dreams into reality was solely in my hands, independent of being married or not.

In my quest to achieve the life I had always dreamed of, I was unwavering in my commitment to hard work and dedication. However, what truly fuelled my drive was the desire to create a future for my sons that would exceed all expectations. I wanted them to have countless opportunities and experiences that would open doors they never even knew existed.

One moment can change everything....

From a young age, the passion for health and fitness coursed through my veins. It was a calling that I couldn't ignore. Determined to turn my passion into a thriving business, I took the leap and opened my very own health club in Collie. The days were filled with teaching and working alongside my husband, who shared the same dedication to wellness.

But it didn't stop there. To fuel my dream, I took on a second job during the night, tirelessly packing shelves at Coles.

The long hours and getting as little as two to four hours of sleep a night for five to six nights a week took its toll. Being one of the top packers and youngest in the team, I was assigned the hardest aisle with the heaviest boxes to lift. I would get home in the early morning hours at around 4 am and grab a shower and a few hours of sleep before my day would begin again.

At a challenging period in my life, when my two young boys were only four and six, I made the decision to embark on a fresh start. Recognising that my marriage was facing difficulties, I took the courageous step of relocating with them to the vibrant city of Perth. It was a significant transition, marking the beginning of a new chapter as I wholeheartedly embraced my role as a dedicated single mother, raising two wonderful boys.

I successfully navigated the corporate hierarchy and flourished in this realm. My hard work enabled me to provide my boys with the life I aspired for them. As I dedicated myself further, my income soared, allowing me to offer them even more.

At the age of 21, Shannon made the bold decision to move to Melbourne and pursue a career as an Interior Designer. Three years later, at the age of 24, he took another leap of faith and relocated to Shanghai to further his professional journey.

Tristan's journey as a Youth Pastor began at the age of 17, fuelled by his unwavering passion for helping children and young adults facing difficult circumstances. Tristan was determined to make a positive impact and to let those who were struggling with drug addiction, experiencing abuse or lacking a stable home life know that they were valued.

As a parent, there are few things that bring greater joy than watching your children grow into remarkable individuals. I have had the privilege of witnessing my two sons blossom into confident and compassionate young men, and it fills me with an overwhelming sense of pride.

Our journey through life has been nothing short of extraordinary. We have experienced moments of love, laughter, and an unwavering display of affection that has strengthened our bond as a family. From the early years filled with scraped knees and bedtime stories to the pivotal moments of their adolescence, we have navigated life's ups and downs together.

Love has been the foundation upon which our family is built. It has guided us through challenges and celebrated our triumphs. Through every milestone achieved, I have seen my sons embrace their passions with determination and enthusiasm. Their growth as individuals has been awe-inspiring to witness.

Laughter has also played an integral role in shaping our journey. Our home was always filled with shared jokes, playful banter, and infectious giggles that permeated every corner.

But perhaps what sets our family apart is the open display of affection we have always embraced. Hugs were never in short supply, kind words were spoken freely, and "I love you" was a mantra woven into the fabric of our daily lives. This open show of affection created an environment where trust thrived, and emotional connections deepened.

I was at home, working with a business partner. He had just left when my phone rang. It was Brisita, Tristan's fiancé. "I don't want to worry you, but I wanted to let you know that Tristan is missing. I've already called the police, and I'm not sure if you'd like to come over to Tristan's house."

“I’ll be right over”, I replied.

I promptly reached out to my husband, Paul, who happened to be attending a conference at that time. Although he was eager to rush over to Tristan's and support me, I wisely advised him to remain at the conference, assuring him that I would keep him well-informed as soon as there were any further developments.

As I made my way down the freeway from my home to Tristan's house, a mixture of anxiety and anticipation filled me. The familiar 40-minute drive seemed longer as my mind raced with thoughts and emotions. A knot formed in the pit of my stomach, and an overwhelming sense of unease took hold of me.

As soon as I reached Tristan's place, I was warmly welcomed by one of his close colleagues who appeared visibly concerned. Showing great kindness, she guided me to the lounge area and mentioned that Brisita was in the kitchen, while also informing me that the police wanted to have a private conversation with me. Shortly after, the authorities arrived and introduced themselves.

In a challenging situation, I was overwhelmed with a multitude of questions from the police that seemed to come from all directions. As panic started to take hold, it became increasingly difficult for me to process the situation and provide coherent answers. This made it even harder for me to think clearly.

During my encounter with the police, they momentarily stepped outside to attend a phone call, leaving me on my own. Upon their return, the young police officer displayed genuine concern.

The next words I heard were, "I'm sorry, but we have found your son. He is deceased."

The piercing sound of agonizing cries filled the air, resembling the painful wails of a fierce creature. To my horror, those desperate screams belonged to none other than myself.

My beloved son had taken his own life.

My entire world collapsed in that one moment, that one phone call, that one day.

In a state of panic and feeling completely isolated, the police officer kindly offered me the opportunity to reach out to someone for support. Without a moment's hesitation, I swiftly dialled my husband's number. With unwavering commitment, he promptly came to my aid, ensuring that I did not face this challenging situation alone.

Embarking on a difficult task, he gathered the strength to make phone calls that no one would ever want to make. With a heavy heart, he started by informing Tristan's father, brother Shannon, dear family members, and close friends of the painful news.

Upon hearing the news, Tristan's father and brother were deeply devastated. The distance between them only added to their anguish, with his father residing in Queensland and his brother all the way in Shanghai. Immediate action was taken to ensure that flights were promptly arranged for both to return to Perth without delay.

As Tristan's mother, I was asked to identify his body. How? How can I possibly do this? How can I find the strength to get through this? My beautiful boy, who meant the world to me. I carried him in my womb and gave birth to this precious boy whom I loved with all my heart.

The immediate aftermath was an incredibly challenging and painful time. We were all grappling with overwhelming emotions.

One of the most difficult aspects was dealing with the authorities and their necessary investigations. As suicide is considered an unnatural death, it was imperative that a thorough investigation take place before any funeral arrangements could be made. This process was daunting and frustrating.

I experienced a profound physical and emotional shutdown as I grappled with the excruciating pain that seemed to originate deep within me. It felt as though my heart had been mercilessly torn away, leaving me utterly devastated.

In the stillness of the night, I endured haunting nightmares that left me overcome with emotion. Tears streamed down my face as I lay in bed, desperately searching for solace. Fearing to disturb my husband's rest, I quietly roamed through our home, weighed down by an overwhelming despair for my precious child.

Exhaustion consumed my days, leaving me with no will to push through.

I experienced a profound transformation as a deep sense of emptiness took hold of me, leaving me feeling like a mere shadow of my former self.

Part of me died with my son!

The question of WHY, was too profound.

The torment of "Why did I not realise something was wrong?" "Why did he not call me?"

These questions were driving me insane.

The Constable, who was handling Tristan's case, informed me that for a mother, the suicide of her child is one of the most difficult things to deal with, and many do not recover from it. She was not wrong.

The journey beyond pain....

As a person who has always relied on my strengths and resilience to navigate challenges in the past, I believed that I was handling everything quite well.

Throughout my life, I have never quite enjoyed seeing pictures of myself. However, there was a particular moment that left a lasting impact on me. As I casually glanced at a recent photograph, an unexpected thought struck me like lightning: "Who is this person staring back at me? She seems so heartbroken." It was in that precise instant when I realised how the light in my eyes had faded away, leaving behind an overwhelming sense of sorrow.

It was at this very moment that I had to acknowledge that I was not alright.

I was trapped in a cycle of torment and, regrettably, I directed my pain towards my husband and beloved pets. It was a painful awakening to realise that by hurting them, I was also hurting myself. I understood that I couldn't allow this destructive pattern to ruin both their lives and mine.

I had to find a way to transcend my pain and embrace life once more.

I delved deep into my reserves of resilience and inner strength with an unwavering determination to overcome the depths of despair. I discovered a newfound motivation to embrace life once more, not only for the sake of my loving husband, my son Shannon, and our cherished fur babies, but also for my son Tristan.

Tristan did not take my life. He took his own.

Embarking on the path to healing....

Drawing upon my well-honed research skills cultivated through years of experience in the corporate realm, I embarked on a profound journey of self-discovery and healing following the heartbreaking loss of my beloved Tristan.

I dedicated myself to conducting extensive research on the most renowned experts in mindset, resilience, spirituality, and personal development. I delved deep into their teachings, immersing myself completely to absorb every ounce of valuable knowledge they had to offer.

I read book after book on personal development, trauma, grief, and recovery.

I attended mastermind after mastermind on spirituality, personal development and mindset.

I had the incredible opportunity to learn from the renowned Tony Robbins, who became one of my esteemed mentors. I travelled to attend his empowering events such as Unleash the Power Within and Date with Destiny. During Date with Destiny, which took place in Cairns, Queensland, there was a profound moment when Tony addressed the sensitive topic of suicide. In that very moment it felt as though he was speaking directly to me, and I could deeply resonate with his words.

With each passing moment, the pain I had long kept hidden began to resurface. It was as if a lid had finally been lifted and the emotions that lay dormant within me started to bubble up uncontrollably. Though challenging, I embarked on a journey of self-discovery and allowed myself to fully feel the depths of anguish within my soul. As this raw pain coursed through my being, it ignited a fire within me to heal and find solace.

I was captivated by a thirst for knowledge, constantly seeking to expand my understanding of my grief. Then one fateful day, as I scrolled through my Facebook feed, I stumbled upon an enticing advertisement from none other than Brendon Burchard himself. It was all about his High-Performance Coaching program - an opportunity I couldn't resist exploring further. After exhausting all other options, I found myself thinking, "Why not give this a try?" With that determined mindset, I enthusiastically took the leap and enrolled for coaching with one of Brendon's esteemed top coaches.

I was fortunate to have an extraordinary coach who made a lasting impact on me. Throughout our time together, we formed a strong connection and journeyed through a transformative process of healing. Her skillful guidance and thought-provoking questions played an instrumental role in the profound transformation I experienced.

With utmost determination and courage, I wholeheartedly accepted the challenge at hand, fully confronting my pain without hesitation. I understood that this was the only path to attain genuine joy, lasting happiness, and the freedom to wholeheartedly embrace life once more.

After experiencing a significant personal transformation through Brendon's exceptional style of High-Performance Coaching, I was inspired to take the leap and enroll myself in his coaching program. It fills me with immense pride to share that I have successfully become a Certified High-Performance Coach.

Thrive after grief....

I wanted to make Tristan proud, knowing that his mum refused to give up the fight for her life.

Tristan always had a way of making every birthday, Christmas, and Mother's Day truly special. Each card he gave me was adorned with the most heartfelt messages that brought tears to my eyes. They were filled with genuine expressions of the love he held for me and his appreciation for my strength and resilience in the face of challenges. His admiration for me shone through every word, leaving an everlasting impression on my heart.

Whenever I find myself grappling with the pain of losing my son, I turn to these cards for solace and a connection to his memory. Each heartfelt message brings me comfort and reminds me of the precious bond we shared.

Through the process of moving forward after a loss, we undergo a transformative journey that shapes us into unique individuals. It is vital for us to wholeheartedly embrace this path of self-discovery, as it allows us to unravel the person we are meant to become.

As our perspectives evolve, so does the value we place on certain things. What once held great significance may no longer have the same impact in our lives. It is a natural part of personal growth and allows us to prioritise what truly matters to us now.

I enthusiastically embraced everything I had learned, and it played a pivotal role in my healing journey. It not only guided me towards creating a new identity but also empowered me to discover the best version of myself - my newfound ME.

Introducing "Rebuild Your Power", a program meticulously crafted to empower executives during challenging times. This transformative program is meticulously designed to guide and support those who have faced heartbreaking losses, helping them rebuild their lives with renewed strength and unwavering purpose.

With my personal experience of navigating through grief and finding the strength to heal, I am uniquely equipped to support individuals in their journey toward resilience and high performance. As a certified coach, I have the skills and expertise to make a meaningful impact on people's lives. Let me help you unlock your true potential and achieve lasting success.

For a more comprehensive understanding of everything I provide, from a wide range of products and services to free resources, I invite you to explore my website. You can also join me on my social media channels for even more valuable content. In my bio, you'll find all the necessary links to access the information you're looking for and discover even more offerings.

We have been given one life to live, and it is up to us to live our best life....

I would be honoured to share my most valuable insights with you, hoping to empower you on your own personal journey. These lessons have greatly impacted me, and I believe they can provide guidance and support as you navigate your own healing path forward.

1. *Live for your loved ones!* Though they may have lost their lives, you still can cherish yours. Honour their memory by embracing life to the fullest. Remember, they are always with you in spirit.

2. *You possess a strength that surpasses your own perception!* Take a moment to delve deep within yourself, and you will discover your own extraordinary gifts, talents, and inner strength. Embrace these qualities and move forward with the love of your loved ones in your heart.

3. *Find acceptance in your pain!* Embrace it as part of your journey towards healing. It is through acceptance that the true healing process can begin.

4. *Allow yourself to break open!* Until you release that deep, dark pain, it will remain trapped within your body, impacting your health and overall well-being. Although it may be a painful step, it is incredibly worthwhile. Give yourself permission to cry, to scream, to get angry, and to truly feel your pain.

5. *We don't simply move on from grief!* Instead, we learn to live our lives while still carrying the weight of our grief.

6. *Give yourself grace!* Each of our paths to healing will be different. There is no direct pathway forward. It goes in twists and turns, ups and downs. Love yourself and find comfort on your journey.

7. *The shift must come from within!* That which you seek externally - your purpose, your identity - may one day be ripped away from you. Our true

purpose and identity come from within and are connected to our soul. Find that and you will transform.

8. *Don't live in your story!* For it is just a story; a story that you must find the value. Turn the page to your chapters and create a newer, more empowering story. This is called your book of life...Live it fully.

From my heart to yours!

"Embrace the gift of life by living it to the fullest and honouring every moment." ~ Tracey Chapman

ABOUT THE AUTHOR

Tracey is an Author, and Resilience and Certified High-Performance Coach.

Tracey is a unique coach in her field, as she has personally experienced the painful journey of grief. Her specialisation lies in assisting executive men and women in rediscovering new passion, purpose, and meaning, while also helping them rebuild their lives after facing a devastating loss.

Tracey's signature program, "Rebuild Your Power," will help you surpass the limitations of therapy, self-help, and support groups. In just eight quick weeks, it will empower you to overcome grief, reignite your inner fire, and discover a new life brimming with meaning, impact, and purpose.

Tracey, an Executive Contributor at Brainz Magazine, has been handpicked and invited to contribute due to her extensive knowledge and valuable insights within her area of expertise. She was exclusively interviewed for an article titled "Navigating Grief to Rediscover Power" and graced the front cover of the August 31, 2023 issue.

Tracey is dedicated to fostering a movement called "Thrive After Grief." She believes that our past is just a part of our story and should not define us. Instead, she encourages us to harness our power and create a new narrative that celebrates our resilience and the strength we have gained from overcoming challenges.

Website: https://traceyachapman.com/

Facebook: https://www.facebook.com/traceyachapmanbiz/

Instagram: https://www.instagram.com/traceyachapman/

LinkedIn: https://www.linkedin.com/in/traceychapman2/

JESSICA SMITH

Breaking Free

I found myself after I lost everything that wasn't me. Sometimes you must lose something to find everything. This is how I took control of my life and let go of my fear. When the adversities of life knocked me down, it seemed like there wasn't a solution to be found. What I discovered was more than I asked for. I never imagined how sweet life could be from where I was. Now it's my mission—to be what I was always meant to be and bask in the deliciousness of sharing this knowledge with all who come to me.

After years of disconnecting from who I truly am, there were so many excuses that I told myself justifying my being in such a disconnected place. There were so many events that occurred that just one of them could have crippled me. I was witnessing my father die slowly from an incurable disease while I was simultaneously in an abusive relationship, and I felt I couldn't talk about either with anyone. Living it was hard enough; I didn't want to burden anyone else. My emotional state had frozen over. It was the lowest I had ever been in my life. I knew deep down I was going to have to change it for myself, but I had no idea how. Even at this low point, I knew it was time for me to make a move. So, I did.

I moved 3,000 miles away. I rekindled a long-lost love relationship with my high school sweetheart. A few months later, we went to the courthouse and told no one except our two witnesses. Getting married was a bold move. All I knew was that I wanted to be in love with someone who genuinely loved me. That seemed like what was most important at the time. I had no idea what I was doing, but I felt so much freedom in the knowledge that I had broken away. This was my opportunity to start over. I didn't do it for anyone else but me. And that felt very empowering.

Fast forward a few years and my husband and I were giving it our best shot. In my opinion, neither one of us was ready for marriage; however, we found comfort in knowing that we weren't alone. We bonded through our suffering; this type of love was conditional. I became my husband's primary caregiver, assisting with the aftermath of being a disabled veteran. I never felt burdened to be there for him. I felt honored to care for someone I loved. However, relationships like this are tricky. It's imperative that you fill your own cup too. My cup was slowly draining. I didn't realize how low I had gotten until my body started shutting down.

About halfway through our six-year marriage, I found it difficult to keep up. My duties as his caregiver were becoming daunting tasks. I felt a tremendous amount of guilt for not being able to keep up. I couldn't get sick. I had to take care of my husband. I made a promise to be there in sickness and health. Till death do us part, right? But how long were we going to live like this? Do we suffer until we die? We knew that our time had come to an end. We both chose separate healing journeys.

My mind and body were consumed with sickness, dis-ease and suffering. I felt excruciating pain every second of every day. It was getting harder to wear that mask, presenting that I was okay. The mask was suffocating me.

After going through the divorce, I had lost my stable income and my health insurance. Two weeks prior to me losing my health insurance, my doctors suggested surgery within the next thirty days to avoid permanent nerve damage and loss of function in my left arm. My most recent MRI and nerve test studies revealed that the degenerative disc disease and reverse curve in my neck had digressed into bulging and herniated discs, along with a severe nerve impingement. I was told it would continue to digress without intervention. I looked deeply into the eyes of my loving doctor, who I knew was trying to help me, and I said, "I can't do that. I'm going to have to figure something out, but I can't do that."

A few weeks later, the global pandemic hit. I was alone for the first time in my life. I wasn't sure how I was going to make it all work. When I closed my art business, I lost my last stream of income. Everything was in lockdown. And I began to break down.

My body continued to degenerate and atrophy. I felt like I was withering away into nothing. This took "broke" to a whole new level. My mind was racing 1,000 miles an hour every day trying to find a solution. Imagining the worst-case scenario over and over. Am I going to die? Something had to give. I started begging for help from God. I didn't understand what I could have possibly done to deserve this, when all I've ever wanted was the best for everyone. Why? Then I had the idea that maybe this wasn't happening to me but was happening for me. How could this be serving me? What was this teaching me? Maybe I was being prepared for something great. It felt delusional to think this way, but it also felt like relief. This way of thinking felt better, but I didn't fully believe it—yet.

I hit rock bottom. I was drowning in the pits of despair and powerlessness. It was so hard not to notice my current reality and the state I was in. I was scared. All I could do was watch myself deteriorate right in front of my eyes. It wasn't just me; but everyone in my life was at a loss as well. My family and friends hurt for me. The doctors didn't know what to do for me. Everyone was just trying to help with the symptoms, but no one had a real solution. I felt so helpless and weak, but deep down, I knew I was not.

There was something inside of me that knew I wasn't supposed to be like this. My spirit was speaking to me, even though I could only hear a faint whisper. That whisper felt like hope. With nothing more to lose, I made a decision. If I had to live with all this pain and anxiety, I could at least change how I felt about it. Thinking about how sick I was only made the pain more excruciating. It's unbearable when you sit alone, and you can hardly feed or bathe yourself because the pain never stops. It almost seemed like it would be easier just to give up. But I'm not a quitter. It's not in my blood. I had survived 100% of everything that I'd been through, and I owed it to myself to prove how powerful I really was. With nothing more than a glimmer of hope, knowing that my spirit was strong, I relinquished my resistance to change.

"If I'm so powerful, show me!", I eagerly declared. I might not be ready, but I'm getting ready. I knew that it was up to me and that no one could do this for me. I had to give all of everything I had left back to myself. From what I understood about energy, I knew I had to stop doubting myself and my ability to heal. I constantly reminded myself to let go of any feeling that wasn't serving me well. Who I was at that time is a reminder of how powerful I am and how far I have come. I will never forget what it felt like to be in that place, but I do forgive myself for being there. At that time, I really did believe I was doing my best. I had no idea how much I was cutting myself off from my own well-being. I now know that this contrast served me well. It doesn't matter how low you go; there's always a way back up.

They weren't tests; they were lessons. Although it didn't feel like I was learning, it felt like I was unlearning. I was allowing—instead of resisting—this so-called stream of well-being that I was told flows to me endlessly. If there really was this abundant stream, I wanted to tap into it. So, I let go and let God. I had to believe there was a solution to all my problems before ever seeing the physical evidence of that solution. It had never been done before, but I was going to do it. I decided to believe in what seemed impossible. I told myself "I am well". I let go of the fear and decided to trust that I was way more powerful than I was aware of. If I were to get into an allowing vibrational state, my body would heal itself. All I had to do was become an energetic match for the healthy person I visualized myself to be.

Once I fully grasped this concept, it seemed too easy. However, I was extremely intrigued. I figured I might as well. What did I have to lose? Let's just try it and see what happens. The more I practiced the vibration of healthy, the better I started to feel. Imagine that. I believed I could, before I knew how I was going to. Then it happened.

I felt the shift and remembered who I was. I'd like to share with you cherished words from my father that I kept close to my heart while I was experiencing my own moments of dis-ease. After 10 years of living with ALS, he wrote a letter titled "I am me". To me, it's an expression of how he found life purpose through his extreme adversity. He ended his letter with this empowering statement:

"My spirit soars, and my life is perfect even though those around me cannot see how perfect it is. That's just because I am loved and can love in return. I am free because I hope and I fly because my imagination tells me it is possible. Nothing can take my spirit, not even my body that has robbed me of so much. I can do all things. I can feel all things. I can love and embrace and dance through the shadows of time with nothing more than the knowledge that I am more than the sum of my parts. I am me. I am at peace and even though outsiders might not believe me, I am well."

It was time to trust the process. Equipped with unconditional love for myself, I proceeded forward. I'm going to "next logical step" my way through this. I started exploring my talents, some that I didn't even know I had. That's the funny thing about trusting the process: as soon as you open yourself up to your infinite potential, you're no longer closed off to your infinite possibilities. The once seemingly impossible became not only possible but easily acquirable. In moments like this, you're aligned with your most authentic self, which is also in alignment with your spirit. This is where all the magic happens. This is what we came for. We are supposed to feel good. This is our true nature. This is "the work".

A creator must create. Realizing there were a plethora of options for me to choose from, I started with activities I could ease into. My whole house was transformed into a creative arts center. Art therapy was my new favorite thing. I would paint every day, sometimes all day. When I was painting, I knew that I was creating. "No mistakes, just happy accidents," like Bob Ross would say. This was a way to express myself without thinking. I felt nothing at times, and that nothingness was beautiful.

I started to notice longer periods of time where I wasn't focused on my sickness and felt no pain. I was focused on the present. I found that everything I was feeling was between me and myself. Not only would I paint but I would also write. I would make lists of everything that I loved, to refer to when I felt like doing nothing. I wasn't going to allow myself to give up on me. I began writing out everything that I wanted to manifest, as if it had already happened. Embracing the energy of appreciation, I would list everything that I could possibly appreciate. When I redirected my focus towards appreciation, I felt an authenticity come over me. This was who I truly was. I finally started to meet myself. And I loved her. I loved her unconditionally. I needed no reason. I became love, and I was open to giving and receiving it in abundance.

Once I began to trust myself again, I realized it was time to start moving my body and ease myself into an exercise program. I hired a personal trainer and told him nothing about how broken my body was. All he needed to know was that I was on a journey towards wellness. I wanted to be fit physically, mentally, and spiritually. I practiced deep breathing techniques and meditated regularly. Even when I didn't know if I was doing it right, I stayed consistent. I had this belief that I couldn't get it wrong because I'm never done. I'm going to either learn from this experience or I'm going to love it. Those were my only two options.

Over time, I began to see failure as a superpower. It is not failure when you have an opportunity to learn and show yourself how resilient you are. I had nothing left to prove or defend; I just knew that feeling good feels good, and I want more of it. I felt a tremendous amount of ease listening to videos that I would find on the Internet. I became infatuated with learning more about this energy world. Some of the teachers I was most fond of and would regularly listen to were people like

Abraham Hicks, Deepak Chopra, and Dr. Joe Dispenza. The more I studied their philosophies, the more empowered I felt. I knew I could do this. Not only was I going to do this, but I was also going to show other people how to do it too. I felt like I had stumbled upon the golden ticket of life.

With consistent practice of my newfound way of life, I healed. As a result of me redirecting my focus towards well-being, I became well. By no longer allowing my sickness and sorrows to be a dominant vibration, this freed up my focus to redirect towards things that felt good. I became addicted to feeling good. It wasn't just about feeling good; but I was also releasing my resistance. I felt like I was shedding parts of me I no longer needed.

One beloved day, I received the proof. I was right. By getting my life in alignment mentally and spiritually, my physical spine found alignment too. I went to see the neurologist, and this time I brought my mother. The results were in from my recent MRI test. It had been eight months since my last MRI. The anticipation was intense. When he pulled up the results, I kid you not, he said, "This is what I call a miracle". He noted that my spine had reversed back, I had released my nerve impingements, and my discs were no longer bulging. My mother and I broke down in tears. They weren't tears of disbelief; they were tears of belief. Empowered with appreciation, I knew deep down that it wasn't just a miracle. This was an example of deliberate alignment. I did that. It was not a gift, but a God-given skill set; Spirit is always with me. Not only did my body start to heal, I became incredibly healthy. Everything about my life changed. I felt unstoppable. I began achieving new heights in my physical fitness; my relationships improved, along with my own opinion of myself. I wouldn't even call it healing. It's more like unveiling your true self and intrinsic nature.

Living in this new now, I am free. I am empowered, confident, still, and expansive. I am literally living the dream. The dream that I manifested for myself. Being a master of my emotions, I get to choose. Would I rather feel good, or would I rather feel bad? By being in alignment, I get to enjoy all parts of this life experience, the good and the bad. Living a life of non-judgment and unconditional love, I get to be in alignment while guiding others through my example. I love knowing I can feel however I would like to feel, no matter what's going on outside of me. I also know that it is a choice to utilize my abilities. I am so free that I could even choose to suffer. That's true freedom. I now know I would rather be happy. I don't only know it, but I live it. Every time I share my experience, I find more purpose in my desire.

I knew I couldn't keep it to myself. I felt everyone should know these things. Spirit spoke to me and told me to just show them by being it. So that's what I did. I Bee-z it. Everyone started to notice massive transformations in my life, and they were eager to know how I did it. I was just as eager to assist them towards lining up with the best version of themselves as well. How could I not? I believe we can all feel how we want to feel, at any given moment. Sometimes obstacles in life cause us to forget our true power. I'm here to remind you.

Today, I assist women and men in leveling up their lives mentally, physically, and spiritually by mastering their emotional control. I guide them in taking the steps away from suffering and towards wellbeing. My Creative Connection coaching programs provide a clear, step-by-step strategy designed for one's personal desires. We can connect over the phone, the internet, and/or in person.

Remember, you must fill your own cup first before you can give to others. Do it for yourself, and everyone else reaps the benefits too. When you embody the energy of who you are, without all the resistance, you have an enormous amount of peace and emotional stability that you can take with you for the remainder of your life. Our emotions help guide us towards what we desire. Not only will you start tapping into higher levels of bliss, but when things don't go your way, you're still okay. Not only are you okay, but you are in love with the contrast that life throws at you, because this is an opportunity for you to learn and show yourself how powerful you are.

The results of my clients continue to amaze me, even though I'm fully aware of how capable they are. I never get used to seeing someone change their life for the better and not have it inspire me deeply. Working with my clients is a win-win situation. Not only do I get to be a part of the journey and assist in the empowerment process, but I also get to reap the benefits of witnessing their accomplishments. This is priceless. To uplift and inspire people to know how powerful they truly are by teaching them how to connect to their well-being is an honor. Realizing the profound impact I've had on the lives of others, I derive strength from the expression of their true authentic selves. I am blessed beyond measure to know that my influence is a precious gift. I get to instill in others the strength to continue their journey with grace and unwavering trust in their divine abilities.

Go confidently in the direction of your desire. You have the power to attract anything you desire, if you don't doubt it. Let these words resonate deeply within your soul: You can, and you will. I hope this message touched your heart and inspired your spirit. We really are all in this together. When one of us heals, the whole world heals. You are an important part of this world. Know that you are a powerful, deliberate, creator, and how you feel matters most. What is, is old news. What is, is not how it has to continue to be.

Go forth, knowing that it's up to you. Honor your own well-being and self-worth. To align with your most authentic self, you must accept who you truly are. This is your responsibility; no one else can do this for you. That is a good thing. No one knows you better than you do. You are not your body; and you are not your mind, you are pure spirit in physical form. I hope you not only found inspiration, but also take this as an invitation to change your life.

I'd like to take a moment to appreciate you for aligning your energy to receive this message. May we keep the gift of giving and receiving flowing in abundance. Thank you for just being and being a part of this experience with me. You are loved—unconditionally.

ABOUT THE AUTHOR

Jessica Smith is an empowerment coach, artist, and personal trainer with Creative Connection coaching. She was inspired to pursue a career in self-development after she rediscovered herself, healed, and transformed her life. With a passion for being the best version of herself, she set out on a mission to not only be the most authentic version of herself, but to guide and assist others in creatively connecting to their infinite potential as well.

When you have done the impossible, it's easy to believe in what seems impossible. She teaches how to achieve what seems impossible by creating a successful set of skills that were tested through personal experience. The day she decided to take control of her life was the day that she took control of her emotions. By becoming an emotional master and stepping into her true nature, she was able to manifest a life far greater than originally imagined.

In her spare time, she rejoices in the ability to perform miracles through the path of least resistance, living in a constant state of knowing that we get to choose which direction this life goes; it's all inspiring and expansive. Her purpose is to just be and to be happy.

Facebook:
https://www.facebook.com/profile.php?id=100002487932609&mibextid=Zb-WKwL

Tiktok: @creativeconnection143

Email: creativeconnection143@gmail.com

CATHERINE CABRERA

Trial By Narcissist: Discovering The True Power Of Inner Strength

On the outside, I've had a near-perfect life. I grew up with a loving and supportive family and never had to worry about money or where my next meal was going to come from. While I'll be forever grateful for the opportunities and privileges I had and continue to have, behind closed doors, my life wasn't as carefree as it seemed.

My parents got divorced when I was five years old and I don't remember all that much about that part of my life, but it was the beginning of what would be years of personal struggles. A few years after my parents' divorce, my stepfather entered our lives. He was great. He played games with me and my siblings, taught me how to ride a bike and make homemade pizza, and he made my mother happy. What I didn't know was that ten years later, that same man would completely destroy the life I'd grown to love.

I was 14 years old when he changed, or maybe it was who he really was all along - it's hard to know at this point. His youngest biological child had recently graduated high school and was going off to college when he made the proposition to my mother to retire, move away, and leave me behind. With my mom being the loving and supportive parent she is, she declined without any hesitation; however, it was that interaction that initiated The Change, as we've come to coin it.

The Change started gradually. His demeanor was similar to that of someone who's stressed – he was tense, irritable, hardly spoke to me, and would compulsively clean the kitchen floor (that's how we knew when he was angry).

With me being in high school, I was busy with school, sports, friends and all the normal teenage stuff. Growing up, I had been bullied a lot for my size and that continued in high school. I decided I had had enough of the comments my classmates would throw my way, so I started prioritizing my physical health. I'd go to the gym, go for walks, pay more attention to what I was eating, the whole nine yards. But as my stepfather became more resentful toward me, my approach shifted.

I was working my first job when he started throwing away the food my mom would save for me for when I got home. It would be too late for me to make anything else, so I'd go to bed to be ready for school the next morning. Over time, I got used to eating less and less while exercising more, driven by the positive commentary I'd receive from everyone around me about how I looked. At 16 years old, I lost 65 pounds in nine months.

My eating disorder controlled my life for close to six years and progressively got worse, as they typically do.

During my first year of college, my stepfather snapped. My mom had filed for divorce and tried to protect me the best she could by not telling me things unless she had to, but I learned of his behavior as it got worse. Yelling, throwing away belongings, threats toward her and myself - it was an absolute nightmare and I hated that I wasn't home to protect my mom from the monster he had become.

When the school year ended, I drove to my hometown with all of my belongings from school, having no idea where to call home. My mom had secretly rented a townhouse so I could live there while she gradually moved in, with the hope that he wouldn't find us. We spent nights going through the trash he'd put on the curb to reclaim our possessions, and one night, we found ripped-up notes he'd written with account numbers on them. He was planning to royally screw my mom up financially as if what he was already doing wasn't enough. I was living my life in fear - in fear of the financial implications on my family, the safety of my mom and me, and in fear of gaining weight.

Through all of this, I was eating so little and exercising so much that my body's functionality was decreasing. But to me, it didn't matter - the anxiety controlled my life, no matter how much I refused to believe it. In my second year of college, I started dating someone who encouraged me to live a more balanced lifestyle and to recover from my eating disorder. It was one of the most challenging journeys I've taken, both mentally and physically. Over time, I gained back the necessary weight for my body to function properly.

When I graduated college and started graduate school, my boyfriend at the time and I had been together several years, and he had moved in with my mom and I so we could save some money. What I didn't know at the time was that he was using us. He'd tell me he loved me and wanted to marry me but would also yell at me when I cried and would rarely spend time with me. I knew he was cheating on me, but I was too afraid of being alone to leave him, so I put up with the lies, the panic attacks, being yelled at when I'd cry - I became a shell of a person. He finally broke up with me when he was able to move in with the girl he was cheating on me with. I packed up his stuff like he asked and watched him drive away to fulfill my dream with another woman.

A year later, a friend from college began attending the same graduate school I was at. We started spending more time together and he learned about all the emotional turmoil that had consumed me the few years prior. After a few months, COVID-19 hit, and his living arrangements fell through. My mom was nice enough to offer to take him in so he wouldn't have to leave his job and friends to return to his parent's house. We began dating and were together for several years before he joined the military.

Going into it, I knew it would be difficult, but it evolved into something much worse than I could've ever imagined. While he was at boot camp, I received a message with screenshots of a conversation between him and another woman, making claims that he was dating her. I took it up with him through snail mail - the only option I had due to the communication limitations of boot camp - and he convinced me she was lying. Skipping ahead to the end of boot camp and the start of the rest of his career, he gradually became less communicative and treated me with an immense lack of interest, leading me to feel insecure and anxious about the state of the relationship. However, when I'd bring it up, I was met with "That's a you-problem" and "I'm not your therapist". Over time, I just kept quiet hoping it was a phase, but over the next few months, it only got worse.

I went to visit him for a long weekend, and we spent the weekend together. It felt more like normal, but when I called attention to something I noticed on his phone, it was brushed off, but it bothered me for several days afterward. The next week, I received a call from him, crying, saying that we needed to take a break. I was absolutely devastated and thrown off balance entirely - we had just had what I thought was a great weekend together. I tried to talk to him, but he ignored my messages for five days.

I relapsed into my eating disorder, was having panic attacks multiple times a day, and couldn't function beyond breathing. I spent a month trying to figure out what we could do to mend the damage. I knew it was over but didn't have the heart to face it until I saw his mother post a photo of him and another woman on social media, with all the comments claiming what a beautiful couple they were. Everything from those three years came flooding back - the refusal to post me on social media, the screenshots from another woman, the gaslighting, and my internal sense that something was wrong.

I confronted him and was met with his typical defense: "That's your trauma talking, she's just a friend". But what set me over the edge was the claim that I was emotionally abusive toward him when I had spent almost the entirety of our relationship being made to feel damaged, silenced, and lucky to have someone willing to be with me. Unfortunately, up until that moment when my heart was shattered into millions of tiny pieces, I believed that narrative.

Once that relationship resulted in the dumpster fire it did, the previous three years started to make more sense. I felt abandoned, used, betrayed, and everything in between. I lost myself for the sake of the relationship -I tried so hard to be the girl he wanted me to be that I didn't know who I was anymore, and I had no idea how to find myself again. My mom and my siblings were there for me through it all, but I felt an unbelievably deep void. I wasn't sure I could ever feel whole again. The anxiety was like nothing I had ever experienced before. I was constantly shaky, nauseous, questioning myself left and right over the smallest things. I wasn't just anxious or sad, I was genuinely angry. Angry that someone who knew every little thing about my life would treat me so poorly, lie to me, and go about the world as if being with me was a chore - a role to play to get what he wanted - and I believed the mask he showed me day in and day out.

I made a pact with myself that I would never let him, or anyone for that matter, have that kind of control over me ever again. Instead of dwelling on the breakup and his manipulative and narcissistic behaviors, I shifted my focus to myself and created what would be the best career decision I've ever made.

The week we broke up, I established my own virtual mental health counseling practice, naming it after the very quality I needed to rediscover in myself - Inner Strength. I spent my free time creating the website, setting up consent forms, and sharing my vision with the people I love. Simultaneously, I utilized my newly freed emotional energy to reflect on what I needed to build up my own inner strength to help me heal, not just from the recent breakup, but everything that came before it too.

I had spent most of my life compartmentalizing and pretending I wasn't impacted by these unfortunate experiences, but it only led me to more harmful relationships and negative self-beliefs. I was exhausted from going through the same things over and over again. This realization left me with one question: what would happen if I actually took the time to acknowledge my pain instead of ignoring it?

This very question led me down a rabbit hole of how curiosity and compassion can aid in the emotional healing process. Expanding on my formal education of mental health and therapy, I learned more about the evolutionary purpose of emotions, real-time techniques for challenging the negative self-talk and beliefs that stem from traumatic relationships, and applying the concepts I teach my clients to myself - I know, what a novel concept that they might actually work for me too! Between my own self-exploration and helping clients on their healing journeys, I was starting to rediscover who I really was as an individual person, rather than morphing into whatever I needed to be to fit everyone else's mold for who they wanted me to be.

In all honesty, I learned a lot about myself that I never would've anticipated, including the depth of the pain I had been suppressing for 20 years. The desperation to feel loved no matter the cost and accepting being treated like dirt if it meant not being alone or abandoned. It replayed in every single relationship I ever had - romantic or platonic. I desperately wanted to be loved and have deep connections with people, but was terrified of allowing anyone to get close enough to me because of the pain I assumed they would inflict. Looking back, it wasn't fair of me to make those assumptions, but I can also understand it. The challenge of accepting that reality is what sparked my passion for helping clients work through similar hardships.

Since my ex-boyfriend left, beginning my own practice and, not only working on my own mental health but prioritizing it, I have felt an abundance of love and joy in every aspect of my life. I found my personality again - I'm more confident and secure in my relationships, my career, and my future. I'm genuinely excited when I try new experiences and put myself out there! I'm less anxious, less depressed, and I don't question my emotional stability anymore, partially because I don't have the consistent exposure to toxic and manipulative people - the people I had to choose to let go. Don't get me wrong, the process of letting go was far from easy. It took me a great deal of time and energy, especially the emotional turmoil I experienced in trying to force myself to forgive the people who robbed me of my childhood, sense of worth, and my individuality. In all honesty, I don't forgive them in the typical sense - instead, I've chosen acceptance. I've chosen to accept the sheer fact that these are my lived experiences, no matter how much I hate them, and that I can't change them. I've let go, freed myself from their grip on me, and I've chosen true acceptance to give me the peace I deserve while honoring the depth of emotional turmoil they chose to inflict upon me. I learned the importance of setting boundaries, staying true to who I am and my values, and not settling for less than I deserve. My drive from that point on was to help other people overcome their hardships and move toward acceptance, even if that doesn't include forgiveness.

My dream growing up was to become a therapist, ever since I saw a therapist when my parents got divorced. The safety I felt as she and I played Candyland every week while she spoke to me about the divorce was, and continues to be, my goal with my clients.

For many, the therapy space is the only opportunity they have to express themselves freely and verbalize what goes on inside their minds, and I have the incredible opportunity to be a part of their healing. I get to help clients put words to their emotional experience, talk about and process the pain they feel, and work through it so they can live a more fulfilling and joyful life. I have the honor of learning from my clients as well. They've shown me a multitude of ways that our behaviors can shed a light on how we feel internally, emphasized the strength and courage in vulnerability, and the importance of highlighting wins along the way, no matter how big or small they are! I truly believe that providing a safe and supportive space for my clients has helped me learn how to feel safe with myself as well. It's forced me to practice what I preach and be open-minded, even more so than I already was, and practice the compassion and curiosity I show them with myself.

October 2023 was the first anniversary of Inner Strength Counseling, LLC, the virtual practice I established through my heartbreak. I've started regularly posting blogs on my website to build awareness of mental health challenges, coping strategies, and provide resources for those who may not have access to the services they want or need. The topics addressed include perfectionism, people-pleasing, trauma, anxiety, and eating disorders, with a variety of approaches/questions being answered, as well as how-to's, tips for coping, potential causes or contributing factors, etc. I share snippets of personal experiences mixed in with research, formal methodology, and themes I've observed in sessions with clients (e.g. underlying purpose for people-pleasing behaviors).

My intention for writing these posts was never about notoriety or building my practice directly - my intention was simply to build awareness about the issues and challenges my clients and I have faced and continue to struggle with, and to normalize the difficulty that comes with them. I've been immensely blessed with the opportunity to pursue my passion and to have followed my dream, but it didn't stop there.

In writing my blog posts, I was approached by a magazine that invited me to join them as an Executive Contributor. This involved writing articles and being published in their online magazine!

From there, I met a lovely woman who shared with me that she was compiling stories of women overcoming adversity and invited me to join the publication of the book in the coming months -and you guessed it! - the one you're reading right now is that book!

Having the opportunity to share my knowledge from my formal education and clinical experience was already an absolute dream, but it's been overwhelmingly exciting to be invited to join a platform to share my personal experience and help others feel seen and understood - to know that they are not alone - YOU are not alone!

If you had told me a few years ago that at 26 years old, I'd own and run a successful virtual private practice, be selected as an Executive Contributor for a well-known online magazine and be published in a book - a literal book! - I can guarantee I would've laughed in your face.

I was in a completely different headspace and was content with being complacent. I felt I was in the best position I could be in my relationship, career, and life in general; however, the sad part? I was miserable and didn't realize it yet. When my ex-boyfriend showed his true colors, I thought I was doomed to be alone and unhappy for the rest of my life, but that couldn't have been further from the truth. His leaving was the best thing that ever happened to me. Do I wish he would've approached it differently? Absolutely, but what I went through - all 20 years of being treated like crap - came to a head in October 2022. I was done. Done being treated as less than, done being complacent, done with settling for half-assed effort. I created something I'm proud of, which allows me to continue following my dream by my own rules (aside from ethical and legal regulations, of course!), and I'm in a healthy relationship with someone who encourages me to be my authentic self, no matter how goofy or playful that is. My family has their daughter and little sister back - the real one, not the shell of a person she had been for years.

I think it's pretty clear that while this process has been overwhelmingly positive and exciting, there have been a multitude of difficult lessons too. Learning how to set and enforce boundaries when I hadn't done so previously, staying true to myself even if it means not everyone will like me, and working through my traumas to be able to have a more secure romantic relationship all required a level of energy and emotional discomfort that gave me a new appreciation for the work I do with my clients. I've always known it was difficult, but I was in denial about how much pain and heartache I was holding on to until this point in my life.

Every day, I'm inspired by my clients and the work I've put into my own healing journey, and my hope is to live a life filled with love, empathy, and healing while helping others find their version of that. As one of my clients says, "We can do hard things", and I truly believe every single one of us has the inner strength to overcome even the most difficult of experiences, even if it takes a little extra help from family, friends, or a mental health professional. Realistically, if I could go back and change anything from my life, as difficult as it was for me, I wouldn't. With the help of my family, I learned the importance of empathy, kindness, and love for other people. I learned how to dig deep within myself to overcome my toughest battles. I created a life I love and am excited for while staying true to myself and my values. I found who I really am and who I'm meant to be.

I learned how invaluable and underrated it is to practice what has become my motto: building inner strength through curiosity and compassion.

ABOUT THE AUTHOR

Catherine Cabrera is the owner of Inner Strength Counseling, LLC and a mental health therapist in Virginia. She provides virtual therapy services for people living with anxiety, eating disorders, perfectionism, and people-pleasing tendencies, among other mental health challenges.

Approaching people and challenges with "curiosity and compassion" is the foundation of Catherine's therapy practice, along with the belief that everyone has the inner strength to overcome life's biggest obstacles. She believes every person deserves to be truly heard and understood, and that through this, healing can happen.

Catherine is working toward becoming a Licensed Professional Counselor (LPC) and has completed research on the impact of trauma, anxiety, and relationship dysfunction on a person's emotional and interpersonal experience. This, combined with her personal experience with toxic and abusive relationships, an eating disorder, and overcoming debilitating anxiety allows her to connect with her clients and journey with them toward healing.

Catherine is passionate about building awareness of mental health challenges and shedding light on the importance of curiosity and compassion in the healing process.

Website: www.innerstrengthcounselingllc.net

Blog: www.innerstrengthcounselingllc.net/blog

Instagram: https://www.instagram.com/inner.strength.counseling/?hl=en

Facebook: https://www.facebook.com/people/Inner-Strength-Counseling-LLC/100087326201073/

DR. ALEXANDRA MCDERMOTT

I Finally Know Who I Am And I'd Like To Introduce Myself

When I wrote my story, Reframing Despair: Going From Stuck to Unstoppable, in *Fearless Female Leaders*, I was recovering from uncoupling from a 25-year toxic marriage, managing an undiagnosed chronic medical condition, and rediscovering the parts of myself that had been kept hidden for years. I had just begun stepping into my power. I was engaged in deep reflection, and still am. I was in the midst of deciding which parts of myself I wanted to keep and which parts of myself no longer served me. In writing this chapter, I am chronicling for the first time, for myself, who I am. *I finally know who I am, and I would like to introduce myself.*

My "NewMe" Mindset

When I shared my story in Fearless Female Leaders, I ended it with the posture of the proceedings in my divorce with my soon-to-be ex-husband. This was back in April. We have finally come to an agreement, and our papers are in front of our judge. By the time you read this, I will have had my "Free to Just b." epic divorce party celebrating my new, uncoupled life. I intend to write an entire book about separation, divorce, reframing, and how to get to the "NewMe" mindset. For now, I will simply say that there are innumerable challenges that come with finally walking away from a long-term relationship, especially when you're married with children.

It is multi-layered. You need to move quickly from an emotional state to a logical one, especially if your partner has already moved on, and in my case, likely several years earlier. Otherwise, they have what I term a "divorce-edge" in the proceedings, from a purely business and transactional standpoint. They can manipulate you through your emotions and nostalgia. The sooner you are able to reframe it for what it is now—the "that's mine, this is yours"—the better able you are to come to an equitable resolution. You can then focus your energy on things that matter—like creating a vision for your new beautiful, happy life—done entirely by you, for you. Your life, by design.

Becoming a Bricklayer

Going through transitions in life, any really, brings out people's true essence. These transitions also show you who stays, who gets benched, and who gets exited. You need to become a bricklayer. For me, it is instinct. I know when being around someone doesn't feel good. Maybe it is their energy, snarky comments, or how they treat other people. I start to lay some bricks and create a healthy distance. I try to maintain some space. I am protecting my energy. My philosophy is that I have one life. I intend to live my life with people who are positive, bring me energy, and love me for who I am—the good, bad, and everything in between.

I have an exercise that I do called the Life Boat Exercise. It is something I did with my students when I was teaching in the Organizational Change and Leadership doctoral program at the University of Southern California. The background is this: you will be put in a raft in the middle of the ocean with unlimited supplies and no awareness of a date of return. You need to choose three people with whom you may spend your remaining days. The rules are that you can only select one family member, and the other two people can only be from a specific category in your life. So, if you choose a person from your professional life, you cannot then choose two of those people; you must choose another person. They must also presently be alive.

I conduct this lifeboat exercise quarterly. I want to examine the relationships in my life. I want to take accountability for the connectedness I am bringing into those relationships as well. If I didn't select someone for the boat, am I showing up in their life the way I should be, and if not, how can I show up for them more? In conducting the exercise, it may inspire you to take action and create boundaries. This is the intent. Boundaries require you to have difficult conversations, often with people you love. In my case, I had many conversations that were difficult. I explained my need for love and support. For a little while, I noticed changes in behavior, and then the behaviors would revert back.

My goal in having conversations with the people I love is never to change them. I don't believe in that—you can't make a cat a dog. However, if someone's behavior is hurtful and being around them impacts you in a negative way, then you must make changes to protect your energy and your peace. I have often heard people say, and I agree, that when you examine the five people you spend the most time with, you are the sixth. You want to ensure those people are high-energy, positive people, who are supportive of you and your vision for a beautiful life. If they are not, you need to either bench them or exit them.

Forgiveness is Radical

Of course, I have done my fair share of research on forgiveness. In this case, I will share the meaning of forgiveness from the Greater Good Science Center at UC Berkeley, which says: "Psychologists generally define forgiveness as a conscious, deliberate decision to release feelings of resentment or vengeance toward a person or group who has harmed you, regardless of whether they actually deserve your forgiveness." What I like about this definition is the fact that forgiveness centers on the one doing the forgiving and does not rest on the offense or any sort of gravity of the harm.

In the forgiveness research realm, the importance of forgiveness is key. It acts as a release of the toxicity you are feeling about the offense, but it does not mean that the forgiver forgets or condones the behavior. It just means it's time to simply move on.

In my case, my divorce was nothing short of traumatic. A life I knew for 25 years was upended without warning, and I had to pick myself up and figure it out while fighting every step of the way. Sometimes, and it depended on the day, I had no idea what fight would present itself—a legal battle, a serious medical issue, my soon-to-be ex-husband, his girlfriend, or something with one of my six kids, or their health. Information was manipulated. I was continually threatened and blackmailed—covertly and not-so-covertly. Money promised was withheld. Attempts to literally make me homeless and penniless ensued.

I often used to sit and wonder what made my ex so angry and why I was his target. I have tried every sort of forgiveness program, from radical forgiveness to meditations and so on. I have analyzed this deeply. I have concluded one thing: for me, forgiveness gave way to apathy and forgetfulness. I simply cannot remember a good time we had together. My memories of the past several years with him have taken over and I have nothing heartwarming left. I reframed to see my ex only one way now, as a business transaction. We are rearing children together—beautiful twin girls. The only thing I care about is that he shows up as a father to them and that he tries to be the best father he can be.

What I finally came to understand about forgiveness is that it is the outcome really. I need to let go of all of the harmful, cruel acts that were aimed at me as the target. It doesn't mean that the slate is wiped clean or that I forget everything, let me tell you, far from it. It just means I moved on, and what happened has no impact on me anymore. I am now able to release myself from that life, that energy, and that toxicity and show up in the world the way I was always intended to—soul first, heart forward, unapologetically. I am now "Free to Just b".

The Importance of Mindset and Non-Agendized Love

I see a bevy of doctors and holistic medical providers. Over the years, I have invested a small fortune in uncovering what's going on with my health, including obtaining my own Certificate in Integrative Health and Nutrition so I can better understand the mind-body connection. I may have a specialist for each organ now; I haven't counted. I joke with some of my adult kids that eventually they may have to take me out back. Some laugh, some don't. I am keeping a watchful eye on the ones who laugh.

Instead of looking at myself in the mirror every day and wondering, what if? I tell myself that they've got this, and I'll stay in my lane and show up when they tell me. A year ago, my mindset was different, which no doubt contributed to my many moments of despair.

When I recently uncoupled in February, I think there was a strange transformation that occurred among people close to me. Somehow, in their eyes, I was rendered fragile (?) and feeble (?) The irony is I handled all of my medical things solo anyway. It became sort of a German Shepherd dog tilt when behaviors around me started to change, and people tried to exhibit control and express their opinions on my medical care. Well, here is where I show up again. I am not feeble, fragile, or any other f-word. Quite the contrary. In fact, I am the strongest I have ever been in my life, and I don't need a partner to shore me up. I am, and always have been, my own strength.

Here is the thing: when people suffer from chronic medical conditions, it is difficult to know who to pull in and share things with and who to keep at a healthy distance. This is also a part of protecting your energy and peace. When people are confused and don't feel well, they often suffer in silence.

A lot of times, doctors don't have the answers, and when you leave their facilities without something specific, it frustrates many people, and the knee-jerk is to say," Well, see, they said nothing is wrong with you." That's not the case, obviously. We just don't have a label for it, and when you can't label something, you treat symptoms, can't get to the root cause, and it becomes a vicious cycle with many more questions than answers.

In my case, people on my journey have expressed a lot of opinions. Let me give you an example: when I couldn't move from my bed (literally, I could not feel my legs at times and my toes would curl up), people would try to tell me I should work out, and that would give me energy. I could honestly write a book about all the stupid things people said to me. Listen, I love feedback. But if you haven't attended any of my medical appointments with me, it is a challenge for me to accept your feedback. If you have an article or research you want to send my way, please do. You know I'll read it with vigor. But if you want to give me unsubstantiated medical advice, or health tips, or even try and tell me I am taking too many pills and that is probably the reason for all my problems, then I'll likely laugh because those pills are what's probably keeping me alive—just ask my medical team. The best thing you can do, if you want to truly support someone suffering from a chronic medical condition, is to stop pushing your agenda and instead show up with love for the other person. A simple question, like how can I best support you, is amazing.

Choose Happy

You can choose happy.

Yes, there is debate about this if you let your fingers do the walking through the internet. So, let me clear it up for you. In the research realm, it is called "subjective well-being." I'll give you the 30,000-foot view. Freud was wrong. Hard stop. Now, we have come to learn that even though our genes are somewhat configured with respect to our set point of happiness, for example, my son loves music from a specific male artist that I absolutely abhor, and it sort of makes my ears bleed, so when we take long car trips, I give in; his happiness score is much higher than mine. This is the subjective piece. Here is another example: I would get total pleasure from petting every dirty dog in the world while, others may think I was totally out of my mind. So, our scales of subjective well-being—the things that bring us upticks—are different, because we are different.

Just look at the famous study of the twins. It is akin to the same thing. Genetics determines about 50% of our happiness set point. The rest is up to us—that is great news! So, it is up to you to figure out the other part and let the research guide you, because there are a lot of things you can do to help yourself on your journey. If you want to learn more about it, there is a bevy of research out there, and so many people are showing up now. You can start with Dr. Ed Diener, the Happiness Journal, or even Dr. Robert Holden with his Happiness Index (an assessment you take). There are assessments, tips and tricks, and many things to help you—you can smile, exercise, dance, and even hug someone.

So, choose happy.

I decided to embark on a road to happiness and make it part of my life plan. I wanted to leave Despair, with his lack of fashion sense, at the door, where he belonged. I was done carrying him on my broken back. He had no place in my life, so I bid him *adieu*. I will admit, though, that he pops in now and again. But he doesn't stay. I laid my bricks, and he has been exited.

I am happy to report that I am the happiest I have ever been in my life. But this required work and deep reflection. I had to work through the parts of myself that were ugly, didn't serve me, and kept me stuck for years. I worked through shame, guilt, and deep-seeded flaws. I had to take accountability for creating a life that I allowed myself to stay stuck in for years. I still reflect every day. I work on myself every day.

What I have come to learn are three truths at this point that serve me. I also know that I am flawed. I don't aspire to be perfect anymore. In fact, I feel free to talk to people about my brokenness, like the way I am here, so that we can become more connected to each other and help each other rise. It is that vulnerability that is the key to healing, not just for me, but for anyone who may also feel like they are on an island, like I did for years. I prefer to be *fragmented-me*. My cracks allow people to get close to me, inside, where they feel it too. Otherwise, we would all just show up as walls, and walls are stiff, angular, and immovable—walls can't hug each other or help each other rise.

Three Universal Truths

Through my reflection, research, reading, and writing, I have come to rely on three universal truths that serve me well now. These didn't come to me immediately, of course. Frankly, they came through a lot of journaling, reflection, and sleepless nights. I also believe we can only handle a few pieces of knowledge, or mantras, at one time. So I've narrowed mine down to just three.

The First Universal Truth: You Can Only Control Your Own Behavior, No One Else's.

Throughout the course of my life, that is until now, I have always put others' needs first. I tried very hard to support, mentor, guide, coach, motivate, influence, and focus on others and their needs, well-being, and happiness. I have given in more times than I can possibly count, and eventually, I simply gave up. I lost myself in the labyrinth of toxicity and "everyone-else-ville" by simply bending to the will of doing everything I thought I should be doing to make everyone else happy. What I should have been doing instead was focusing on filling my own bucket and being the best me I could be to serve others.

I finally realized and concluded, through much self-reflection, that even though you can be well-intended, the only person's behavior you can control is your own, no one else's. When you understand and practice this, it gives you immense personal freedom. You begin to conserve your energy, which is yours to keep or give away. You realize that even though you may always be an influence in other people's lives, inevitably, it is their choice how they wish to show up in the world. At the end of the day, if you did your best, you could put your head on the pillow at night, and rest easy.

The Second Universal Truth: "The only constant in life is change"- Heraclitus.

I have heard this explained by others as "This too shall pass"—both the good and the bad. In essence, don't cling to anything. I am not sure I love this frame as much. It tends to favor a negative connotation for me. But I understand and appreciate its essence. When you realize that, in life, you really need to be agile, flexible, and act more like a palm tree, than an oak tree, you begin to understand that no matter what, you can inevitably handle anything life throws your way. You begin to realize that most things, even the most formidable challenges, are actually foreseeable. When you strengthen your mind, by working on your mind muscle every day, by reading, writing, and practicing daily gratitude, the things that would have been big aren't as big anymore. You are able to handle things with grace, head-on. You can protect your energy, set boundaries, and bounce back more quickly. Things just won't hurt you like they used to, and not because you are cold, but because you have stepped into your power.

The Third Universal Truth: You Are What You Believe.

You are unique. There is no one in the world like you. People will show up in all corners of your life and render opinions, give you labels, and tell you who you are and aren't. These may be well-intentioned and maybe they aren't. Even so, they are limits on who you are, because only you know who you are. At the end of the day, what matters is what you believe. You are accountable for the life you lead. Just you.

The choices you make are yours, just yours. Make them with foresight and with intention. Create the life of your dreams. Dream it. Plan it. Live it. No one else's opinion matters but yours. When I was younger, I always had the mindset that if someone thought I couldn't do something, I would prove them wrong and do it. Now, I am different. It is not about them; it is about me. Do I want it? Does it serve me? Is it part of my life plan? If so, not only will I do it, I'll probably do it twice.

Living My Best Life

The life I led and the one I lead now are in stark contrast. I am now living the life designed by me, for me. It is the vision I created for myself. I am no longer bending to the will of others and putting their needs before mine. Don't get me wrong. No one would ever describe me as selfish, but I am now able to put my energy into fulfilling my purpose with intention.

I am truly the happiest I have ever been, but it took work and commitment. I moved to a state I love, near my family. I have made significant changes to my support circle. I am surrounding myself with high-energy, supportive, positive people who are aligned with my values and goals, who love me for me. I pivoted in my career so I could better leverage my strengths and abilities and serve others in the process. I love what I do because I connect with amazing people every day from around the world. I get to hear about their lives and how I can help make their dreams come true.

I wake up with a smile every day and a song in my heart.

ABOUT THE AUTHOR

Dr. Alexandra McDermott (Ali) is a bestselling published author, award-winning global leader, CEO of Pen Crown Publishing and McDermott Leadership, motivational coach, and speaker.

Ali recently framed 2022 as the most transformative year of her life when her purpose became clear: to help people discover their purpose and lead the life of their dreams.

She has been published in several genres, coached global leaders to go from stuck to unstoppable, and is now devoted to her life's purpose.

Ali will be published in several books this year as well as coach others on how to share their messages of inspiration and empowerment with the world in both collaborative and full-length books. Ali's full-length book, Free to Just b., will be released in the spring of 2024.

Ali thrives on connectedness, so please feel free to connect with her on LinkedIn.

As an international book publisher, Ali helps others share their messages with the world. She has a special surprise for her readers, which can be found on her website.

Website: https://www.PenCrownPublishing.com

Website: https://www.McDermottLeadership.com

Amazon Author Page: https://www.amazon.com/author/dralexandramcdermott

LinkedIn: https://www.linkedin.com/in/alexandramcdermott-innovation-management-leadership-venturecapital-entrepreneurship-ai/

LUNA STARFEATHER

A Taste Of My Own Medicine

"*Incurable*". "*Irreversible*". "*Permanent*". And my personal favourite: "*There's nothing we can do.*" These were just a few of the terrifying programs I was fed by doctors and so-called "experts" upon receiving diagnoses for three separate health conditions, all before the age of thirty. But their truth was not my truth. Just because there was nothing *they* could do, did not mean there was nothing that could be done. And thus began my decade-long, epic exploration of just what *I* could do.

From as far back as I can recall, I had always held a keen fascination for how things worked: the human body, the natural world around us, even how a kite remained up in the sky. I guess you could say I was born a natural Science Geek. I had this unquenchable thirst for knowledge, for figuring out the *why* and the *how* of everything within and around me.

My father was the same. Something of a mad scientist himself, my dad enthusiastically indulged my scientific hunger by gifting me every science kit you could possibly imagine from an exceedingly young age.

While my older sister would while away hours playing with Barbies, my father and I were growing copper sulphate crystals with my chemistry set, building electronic circuits to turn on a light bulb, fashioning a radio, making iron filings dance with giant magnets, or examining the complex wings of a crane fly under my microscope and exploring the structural differences between igneous and sedimentary rocks.

I could not get enough, and not only did my father both encourage and nurture this captivation, but science appeared to be the first love we shared that primarily bonded us. It brought us together and cemented our relationship from then onwards. Science would remain a deeply ingrained part of my being, which, unbeknownst to me at the time, would come to play a vital role in my healing journey, a journey that began around the age of twenty-three, when I experienced the first of three momentous occasions of Reckoning.

During a lost period of post-graduate confusion, finding myself in a soul-sucking, corporate, sedentary desk job for the first time in my previously highly active and sporty life, my back suddenly went out, quite literally bringing me to my knees. I found myself, for the first time ever, in perpetual nerve pain to the point of paralysis. It was not only excruciating, but utterly terrifying. I was trapped in my body. I could not move. And I appeared to have no control over it whatsoever.

Following an MRI scan, the consultant orthopaedic surgeon explained to me that I had a deformity in my lower spine, which he showed me on the x-ray. He declared it to be “Inoperable”, “Irreversible” and “Permanent”, and went on to inform me that there was absolutely nothing that could be done, that I would most likely be in pain forever, and that my only course of action was to take painkillers every day for the rest of my life.

Now, if I had been some other impressionable and innocent young person, I may well have taken that information as a given medical *fact*, followed that “expert guidance”, and proceeded to carry that incepted belief in my apparent lack of power for the rest of my doomed life. Fortunately, I am not that person, and on receiving that news, I experienced what I can only describe as a deep and intuitive knowing from somewhere profound inside me.

My stomach sank, and every muscle in my body contracted. My body expressed a resolute and definitive NO! Everything within me told me that this idea did not resonate as truth for me, and what *did*, in fact, resonate as truth was the knowing that I, and everyone else, was able to fully heal myself from anything. I can now appreciate retrospectively how this was my spiritual call to arms.

I demanded a second opinion and was told that Pilates would help me to manage the pain, but I was given the clear warning that I had to practise every single day or else the pain would certainly return. I dutifully practised every day for around seven years; however, the reason I was forced to cease this practice led me to the second Reckoning of the three.

At the age of twenty-nine, following a brutal and ultimately life-changing sexual trauma (the last in a long line of sadly similar events), I received a fateful tick bite during my stay on a Zen Meditation and Mindfulness Teacher Training retreat. (The irony of this is by no means lost on me!)

The further irony is that shortly before this trip, I had launched a clear intention to the Universe that, having been fit and healthy all my life, I now desired to really level-up my health and optimise my wellness. My goal was ultimate freedom.

Being something of a natural manifestation master, a subject I now passionately teach, I was subsequently introduced to the powerful lesson of "Be careful what you wish for".

Within a couple of days of being unwittingly bitten, I developed the signature bulls-eye rash on my leg at the site of the bite, which interestingly turned out to be my saving grace. I began to become suddenly and perpetually unwell, displaying a rather vast and confusing array of symptoms that I was not used to, including frequent and prolonged flu, inexplicable mood swings, brain fog, anxiety, headaches, muscular pains, extreme fatigue, and exhaustion.

There did not appear to be any logical explanation for this sudden decline in my health, but the mysterious rash kept returning. After a long string of misdiagnoses by a variety of doctors, at the age of thirty, a year after being bitten, I finally received my answer. A Lyme-literate dermatologist recognised the rash and diagnosed me with Lyme disease, an autoimmune disease that I had never even heard of, and that was not that well-known in the UK back in 2012.

The treatment he offered me was a month-long course of antibiotics, which I gratefully accepted, ignorantly believing that this would be the end of it, just like with any other bacterial infection. Unfortunately, this did not prove to be the case, because with Lyme disease, there is only a short window of seventy-two hours in which antibiotics will have any remedial effect, and it had been almost an entire year for me since my bite.

Not only did these pharmaceuticals consequently prove to be entirely futile by way of treatment, they produced an extreme response in my body known as a Herxheimer reaction, exacerbating all the symptoms and rendering me bed-bound for six months with full-body inflammation, the most extreme case of flu I have ever experienced, high fever, and the inability to move my entire spine, head, or eyes. Once again, I found myself trapped in my body, unable to move, and terrified.

My "Science Brain" jumped into action and propelled me into a furious rampage of research from my sick bed, demanding that I discover every single detail about Lyme disease in the desperate hope of finding a way through and out. I was shocked by what I discovered.

Every piece of information on the internet confirmed that this was an "Incurable", "Irreversible", and "Permanent" condition and that there was no known cure anywhere in science. When my eyes fell upon those words, a familiar feeling returned. That sinking sensation in my stomach and the contraction of every muscle in my body—that indisputable NO! And I now fully understood where that voice was coming from. It was my Soul.

My all-knowing, wise, infinite, omniscient Soul was communicating with me through my body, reminding me of my truth: the truth that no matter what the internet, doctors, or *anyone else* said for that matter, it was indeed possible for me to heal myself—fully and permanently. I just knew it.

I also knew something else at that moment. I knew that not only was it my mission to find a way to heal myself permanently, but that it was also my calling to inspire and facilitate others to do the same for themselves. I have always believed and known that we are built to self-heal, and that there is no body that is so sick that it cannot be healed back to wellness. It was just a case of finding the way. And thus began my mission from my sick bed, where I spent the best part of the next ten years.

I spent those first six months in bed poring over every piece of information I could find about Lyme disease, autoimmune disease, and functional medicine, and eventually I discovered an amazing functional medicine expert in North Carolina called Dr. Bill Rawls, who gave me my first glimmer of hope. A doctor and fellow Lyme sufferer, this incredible man created a company called Vital Plan, which assists autoimmune sufferers in the recovery from conditions such as Lyme disease and fibromyalgia.

I began importing healing herbs from the United States, radically changed my diet, and followed the holistic protocols offered. Within three months, my symptoms had abated.

As grateful as I was to finally have some relief, I admit to having felt somewhat unsatisfied with this long-term prognosis.

Much like with the Pilates treatment, I understood from what was explained to me that if I religiously maintained my daily dose of herbs (which incidentally totalled at about thirty-six capsules per day), then my symptoms would remain at bay. Meaning that if I were to stray from this protocol, my symptoms would no doubt return. The idea of being dependent on something *outside* of myself for my sense of well-being filled me with dread and an overwhelming sense of disempowerment.

This just wasn't enough of a solution for me. Call it perfectionism if you will, or call it simply an inner *knowing*, but I was determined to find a permanent answer or cure for this condition. Having to accept that I had a lifelong condition that I would simply have to embrace and manage just did not sit well with me. In fact, it just simply did not resonate as truth within me at all! It felt like the polar opposite of *freedom*. However, the plot then, as they say, thickened.

Upon receiving the devastating news that my father had leukaemia, the emotional stress triggered an autoimmune response in my gut, causing me to develop severe rectal bleeding and inflammation, something I had never previously experienced. This brings us to Reckoning Number Three: my diagnosis of ulcerative colitis at the age of thirty-two.

This is where things begin to get really interesting, because the prognosis and treatment I was offered by the doctors for this condition was a toxic cocktail of lifelong medication. I was instructed to take a daily prescription of high-dose anti-inflammatories and immunosuppressants every day for the rest of my life, for both remedial and preventive purposes.

Naturally, I questioned how on earth I was supposed to manage my Lyme symptoms while under the power of immunosuppressants, because the necessary treatment for Lyme disease, I had discovered, proved to be keeping my immune system boosted as much as possible. This new introduction of suppressing my immune system to manage my colitis appeared to be completely counterintuitive to everything I had worked for over the past two years to achieve any semblance of wellness.

Every question I asked was met with the same hopeless response: "I'm sorry, I don't know." And they didn't. This was not something they had ever been presented with before. All they could tell me was that my condition was, you guessed it, "Permanent", "Incurable" and "could and *will* return at any time", and therefore it was essential that I remained on medication forever or else I would inevitably have to have my entire colon removed. This is what I was told as "medical fact."

Having grown up with an older sister who was a chronic Crohn's sufferer, I had witnessed first-hand the agonising battle with inflammatory bowel disease, so I had no reason to dismiss the doctor's advice or guidance. And yet, I could not shake off that persistent little voice within me, that insisted I would find a way to absolute health, in line with my intention those years before.

So I found myself on my own, in an impossible dichotomy. How could I begin to navigate my way through these two opposing conditions, both of which had entirely contradictory diets, protocols, and medications that counteracted one another? Once again, "Science Brain" jumped at the challenge.

Finding myself bed-bound for a further six months in total agony, without the option of any pain relief, trapped with nowhere to go, I immersed myself in voracious research, cross-referencing everything in my dogged attempt to find anything that I could eat, drink, or supplement to keep myself alive and well, while not interacting with anything I had been prescribed by the doctors.

By this stage, I was at a point of starvation, unable to take any food at all, living on nothing but clear chicken broth and herbal tea, which was not a safe diet for the large amounts of prescription medication I was taking, but tragically all that my body would allow.

The doctors put me on several, long rounds of steroids that contained a number of recorded side effects I had the pleasure of experiencing, amongst which were: unwanted hair growth, unwanted hair loss, extreme weight gain and bloating, nausea, increased appetite (which was unfortunate as I could not eat!), violent mood swings, extreme rage, weepiness, depression, insomnia, and eventually, as per the warning on the box, psychosis.

Coming from a place of extremely strong mental health and a natural disposition for positivity, this came as quite a shock. Furthermore, these legally prescribed drugs led to the first of several occasions where I almost died during this healing journey. But that is a story all of its own that I will share another time, in another book.

Suffice it to say, I found myself quite literally fighting for my life. "Science Brain" was at the end of her long and exhausted rope, no longer able to function healthily under the spell of these harrowing psychotics. But now there was nowhere else to turn. So this is where my trusty Soul stepped in and, quite literally, saved my life. Not only my Soul, but my greatest Soul Ally in this life: my mother.

My father's influence had served me well up to this point, and tragically, I lost him to leukaemia in the midst of all this chaos. And now my mother's influence played a pivotal role in my healing, for where my father brought the science, my mother brought the Spirit. An extremely wise and gifted therapist, spiritual healer, and medium, my mother humbly embodies Divine Compassion itself.

When I hit this extremely dark period in which I found myself lost completely to the power of these mind-altering substances, my unconditionally loving and devoted mother, who was by this point caring for me full-time, helped me to reconnect to myself, my divinity, my inner wisdom, and my truth. Day after day, she would patiently sit at my bedside, expertly guiding me through practices to connect with my Spirit, and Soul, and Source itself, because although I was extremely advanced in all these skills, at this point my connection was weak, and my trust in it was even weaker.

During this hazy, Groundhog-Day-style period, I was in a state of perpetual agony and torture on every level: physically, mentally, emotionally, and spiritually. The constant pain was overwhelming, and there was no form of pain relief I was able to take, other than using my Zen techniques of breathing and meditation to prevent myself from passing out constantly. I was not able to sleep as I was running to the bathroom every ten minutes throughout the night as well as the daytime.

Furthermore, I was losing a consistent amount of blood every day from my bowel. I was unable to eat, so I was weak, malnutritioned, and permanently nauseous, and to be perfectly honest, at this stage I suspected I was in the process of dying.

The drugs had forced me into energetic separation from my Soul, and I was hanging on to my grip on reality by a very fine thread. My hope and innate optimism were waning, and despair was setting in. I even experienced an extremely rare moment of defeat and a reluctant yet powerful urge to give up. But my mother never gave up on me. She diligently poured her love and energy into supporting and anchoring me, reminding me who I was and that I was not lost, that everything I needed to survive and conquer was still right here inside of me.

At some point in this repetitive process, my Soul spoke to me, and I had a sudden revelation. I realised that my suffering was being perpetuated by my thirst for control and subsequent frustration at discovering that I truly had none. So what was my alternative? It dawned on me that I simply needed to surrender. Surrender to trust. Trust in my Soul, trust in the Universe, and trust in my destined path.

I really had no other option, other than to give up, of course, and I have never really known how to do that as it is not built into my nature. So I made the choice to do just that—I surrendered. And magically, in that moment of surrender, I felt my first wave of relief, which brought me to instant tears. I can still remember the spot I was standing on in the bathroom in the middle of the night when that "aha!" moment dropped in.

This wave of relief was followed instantly by a surge of power. All of a sudden, I knew what I had to do. Nothing. I had been working, and trying, and fighting so hard, and getting absolutely nowhere. And now it was time to stop and do nothing. Nothing but surrender and trust. I had to come out of my drug-fuelled, chaotic, confused, and fear-plagued head and return home, back to my heart-space, back inside to my inner wisdom, and reconnect to my pure knowing once more. In other words, it was time to stop listening to my ego and reconnect with my Soul. And when I did this, the weirdest and most wonderful thing in the world happened. I started to exponentially heal.

Something became crystal clear to me: once I had surrendered and relinquished the illusion of control, I was then able to access my true *power*. I had mistakenly believed that *control* was the force that was giving me power in this situation, but that was nothing but an illusion.

Once I moved into a space of surrender, quieted my mind from the endless fear-based chatter, and entered my heartspace—the gateway to my Soul—there waiting for me was not only my divine power, but all the answers, guidance, gifts, and healing magic that I needed to fully return to myself and heal. And I did. *This* was my first true taste of Sovereignty.

And this is now what I teach and assist others in accessing for themselves.

A wise friend once told me that there are at least fifteen roads to any healing, and she was right. There is no one-size-fits-all formula because we are all entirely unique beings. But we all possess the wisdom, the power, and the divine gifts, and everything we need inside of us to find our own individual route to healing, or to whatever desired intention we may hold.

All that is required is to quieten the ego, the fear-mind, surrender to your Higher Self, your Soul, Source, the Universe or whatever higher power you have faith in, and tap into that truth and wisdom deep inside that cannot lie to you, that has your very best interests at heart, and that is propelling you forward onto your highest path and purpose. And then listen. And trust it. (Just like I have absolute trust that my Soul chose the perfect parents to assist me on my own path and purpose!)

You then move into your true power and step into the frequency of Sovereignty, where you are no longer dependent on anyone or anything outside of yourself for your own sense of wellbeing, safety, security, self-love, or self-worth. This is the "secret sauce", and I am living, walking proof that this works.

I am now living my very best life, entirely free from disease and medication, enjoying total physical freedom and health. I bridge the two worlds of science and spirituality in my Quantum Healing work in order to help others to truly heal from the inside out, as I did myself. And do you know, that back issue never ever returned. And I have not practised Pilates for over a decade. So much for "medical fact"!

ABOUT THE AUTHOR

Luna Starfeather is a Trauma-Informed Sovereignty Coach, Soul Activator, Manifestation Mentor and Quantum Healer. She is also a Reiki Master and experienced Psychic Medium, having trained in the Shamamic Healing arts from her early twenties.

She combines sixteen years of vast experience in the field of Holistic Medicine where she honed her craft in the Physical, Mental, Emotional, Spiritual and even Soul-Level and Quantum Realms in order to empower people to heal and energetically upgrade themselves, and step into their full Sovereign power.

Luna blends Transformational Life Coaching, Energy Medicine, Inner-Child Healing, NLP, EFT, Zen Meditation and Mindfulness, Belief Clearing, Quantum Healing, Intuitive Guidance, Inner Child Healing, DNA Activation and Soul-Level Blockage Removal to help you identify and permanently clear any blockages to the embodiment of your Full-Potential Self, and bring you into alignment and integrity with your Soul, Higher Self, Intuition, Sovereignty, Self-Love and your Highest Path and Purpose.

Luna runs a 1:1 coaching practice and has just launched her first online coaching program, The Ultimate Sovereignty Quantum Upgrade, which will shortly be followed by her second group program Miracle Medicine, in which she will teach you how to heal yourself naturally from the inside-out.

Facebook: https://www.facebook.com/LunaStarfeather

Instagram: https://www.instagram.com/lunastarfeatherdivinecoaching/

Linkedin: https://www.linkedin.com/in/luna-starfeather-007a5b227/

Website: https://lunastarfeather.com

Linktree: https://www.lunastarfeather.com/link-tree

LYNDA BARRUS

Rising Into Love: A Journey Of Self-worth

From my early years, I carried a deep sensitivity to the world around me, a trait that ultimately led to a pattern of codependency. While it offered comfort, it also shielded me from some harsh realities, leaving me vulnerable to heartbreak and feelings of unworthiness. This emotional landscape paved the way for how I viewed my own self-worth.

Over the course of three decades, the weight of ADHD, executive dysfunction, and a general sense of unease bore down on me. They cast a perpetual shadow, clouding my thoughts with brain fog, sapping my energy, and sowing a profound lack of motivation and an overwhelming feeling of unworthiness. As time passed, these conditions exacted a toll, costing me cherished friendships, eroding my self-worth and self-love, stealing precious moments with my children, and ultimately leading to the dissolution of my marriage.

Despite facing challenges with depression, anxiety, chronic allergies, and the onset of chronic pain and fatigue, my body often rebelled against a variety of external factors. Balancing these health concerns with the demands of an unhealthy marriage and raising two young children, I was determined to pursue becoming a Special Education teacher.

It was a taxing journey, completing both my associate's degree and moving on to my bachelor's degree in Special Education. The years between 2001 and 2006 were marked by moments of feeling out of sync with myself as my marriage faced its own rocky patches. I persevered, wearing a smile as proof that we wouldn't become just another statistic. Finally, in 2006, I graduated and embarked on a new chapter working in a nearby school district as a Special Education teacher.

In April 2007, a surprising pregnancy brought a mix of emotions, and in September, I gave birth to my youngest son. In November of 2007, I noticed pain in my right breast and discovered a lump. In January 2008, I had various medical appointments and tests and received the devastating news of infiltrative lobular carcinoma. The cancer had spread to my lymph nodes, necessitating extensive surgery.

In the midst of my battle with cancer, I grappled with feelings of unworthiness and a profound sense of not knowing who I truly was. Living authentically seemed like a distant dream. There were moments when hope seemed to slip through my fingers, leaving me to call upon a higher power for the courage and support I desperately needed.

Yet, through it all, my resilience and determination never wavered. I faced the emotional toll of cancer treatment head-on, enduring the grueling rounds of chemotherapy and radiation. Simultaneously, I continued to teach and care for my children (as best I could), drawing strength from not wanting to fail, let others down, or ultimately become a statistic. The loss of my hair was a deeply emotional experience, one that still stirs emotions within me.

In those challenging moments, it was for my children that I found the strength to press on. The unwavering support of my close-knit circle of friends and my mother provided me with the motivation and fortitude to keep moving forward, reminding me that I was never truly alone in this fight and that I didn't want to let anyone down.

Despite the support of loved ones, I grappled with moments of loneliness and the weight of the battle. However, my children remained my driving force, reminding me to find the courage to face each day. In the quiet moments of the night, I drew on my inner strength and the love that surrounded me. Yet, amid this seemingly endless struggle, a glimmer of hope emerged, leading me on a transformative journey of healing, self-discovery, and ultimately back to self-love.

Ultimately, I recognized that self-love was a crucial component of my healing journey. I resolved to continue forward, knowing that love for myself and my children would carry me through any storm.

After a few months of chemo treatments, I began to lose momentum and optimism. I was not doing well with allowing people to help. I'd get pissy if they asked me if they could do something, and I'd get pissy if they didn't ask. My ex-husband tried helping with the baby, but he just didn't do it the way I would and used to let him cry longer than I would. I'd get all pissed and just do it myself. I remember reaching out via email to a friend and having a conversation to vent, explaining how I was not only getting short-tempered with my ex-husband but had started taking it out on the kids. I became emotionally drained, disconnected, and verbally abusive.

Chemotherapy went on through October 2008, and radiation started right after and ended in December. I was exhausted, but I kept going. What else was I supposed to do? I worked. I slept. I did what I thought I could with being a mother to my three kids. I had a great support group that I joined. Women and coworkers who helped with cleaning and bringing meals.

I worked and went to treatments on Wednesdays. These days were difficult, but the kids' grandmothers helped out, and my oldest son helped to drive me back and forth.

As each day went on, I became more resentful of life, my ex-husband, and being a mother. What kept me going was something that this cute little old lady—a three-time cancer winner—shared from the book "The Secret". SO POWERFUL. I knew that if I could do my best at being optimistic rather than pessimistic, I could beat this. She shared her thoughts on how it helped her and how she practiced mindfulness and breathing techniques to make it through the down days, the pain, and all the emotions.

It worked to a point, but seemed to be only a Band-Aid as everything caved in around me. BUT I kept moving forward, faking it until I knew I could make it.

Spring of 2009

I was still feeling like I was in a fog from chemo brain (a real thing), and added to that was the momma fog brain. There is not much that I recall from this time.

My relationship with my ex-husband deteriorated. I was verbally abusive and short-tempered with just about everyone. It seemed the cycle continued; the more he isolated and drank, the more short-tempered and resentful I became. I constantly snapped at the kids. I became obsessed with seeking out the signs that he was drinking, all the while avoiding my own need for healing. I finally started attending online meetings for ALANON. Their 12-step program reminded me that I get to be selfish. I remember clinging on to the description of being on a merry-go-round. I couldn't jump off; if I did, I would not know where I would land or who I would be.

Fall of 2011

I often had conversations with myself, trying to figure out what I felt about everything that had happened and asking myself who I was and what my purpose was. I spent hours journaling about my true feelings, asking for guidance, and seeking answers to questions such as: Was I really okay with my relationship with my ex-husband? It had been years since I felt happy, and loved, or that I really came first. Isn't that how a relationship should be? I used to bend over backward to do things to make him happy, but when I never got anything in return, I gave up. I had given up on many things including the dreams I had of growing old with him.

I recall reading an article on what to think about before throwing in the towel. One of the questions was whether you ever really had a true relationship or were just living as roommates. As much as I tried to pretend that we had a true relationship, it had never been there. So there I sat feeling like I had wasted twenty years of my life. Twenty years of unhappiness and false feelings. I had three wonderful children, whom I cared for and adored immensely, but other than that what was there? Kids aren't everything, right? They soon grow up, and move on, and find their own families to love and care for. Then it would just be me.

I have never felt that my ex-husband was there for me through anything emotionally. He was there physically, but I don't think he knew how to reciprocate my feelings. There are so many things that we don't have in common; actually, I can't even think of one thing we have in common aside from loving the kids.

I told him over and over that I was not happy and that I was not happy with his drinking, but I never gave him the entire picture. It always ended up with me crying and him being defensive. It never went anywhere. I didn't know how I was going to gain the strength to actually leave.

I don't think I asked for much. I would have loved to have had someone who asked me what I would like to watch on TV. Someone who would make the decisions on what to eat for dinner. Someone who came home and picked up the messes that were always there. Someone that I didn't have to hound to do chores, which were just part of being a partner and a homeowner.

I felt, more times than not, that I had four kids to care for. I wondered whether we should go through counseling and try to resolve things, or was there really anything to resolve? I was always so short-tempered and irritable with him that he couldn't possibly have been happy. And the more irritable I was with him, the more he drank, and then the more short-tempered and irritable I would be with him.

When I went back to school to get my teaching license, it was to make sure I could fend for myself and the kids. After getting my first teaching job and getting pregnant with my youngest son, things changed for the better. I took it as a sign that everything may be looking up and that we could actually make the marriage work.

After going through the breast cancer treatment and then dealing with the fibro, things had only gotten worse for me as far as how I felt towards him. I cringed when he touched me instead of getting butterflies. He rarely asked to help me, he rarely did things around the house to help, and he was just so negative with his words. It brought me down and irritated the hell out of me.

I felt like a bomb that was ready to go off. Why must I think about his feelings? Why couldn't I be selfish and be done with this? I kept journaling, meditating and asking for answers or a sign of what to do and what is right. I was sick to my stomach and just needed a break from everything.

All I could think about was how everything I had ever wanted had fallen apart or never truly existed. I had tears that wouldn't stop flowing. My oldest son came over to visit, and I couldn't stop thinking of how horribly his life had been ruined because of the choices I had made. Where would we all be today if I had been strong enough years ago to leave my ex-husband or to put my foot down? I wanted to just sleep and not have to think about anything anymore.

My ex-husband was working that day, and there was snow all over outside. My daughter had stayed at my mom's the night before, so it was just my youngest son and I. I had way too much time to sit and think about life. What did I want from life? Was I really unhappy with my ex-husband, or was I unhappy with myself and the choices I had made? A lot had happened over the previous five years, and I honestly don't think that I had allowed myself to grieve properly over losing the old Lynda. I decided to step down as Chapter Manager of Salt Lake City Mommies (SLCM) and just be a member, which would hopefully allow me to truly focus on myself.

I mean, for heaven's sake, I had gone through cancer and then fibromyalgia, all the while continuing to work full-time and consuming myself with SLCM. No wonder I was feeling lost and unhappy. I may have been unhappy with my ex-husband, but the more I dug deep into my own feelings, the more I realized that there was much I needed to work through before I could just say I was done with him.

In August of 2012, I finally had the courage and sense to file for divorce, aware that this should have happened many years ago.

I do know that there was pain and a lot of emotion. At that point, I was on three to four prescription medications. By 2014, I had added ten medications to the list. I had exhausted my PTO and burnt bridges with the principal of my school and many close friends. I remember going to my internal medicine doctor and telling her that I was done with the prescriptions. I wanted to be completely clean and free of them. Begrudgingly, she helped me taper off the medications, and by the spring of 2015. I was prescription-free.

During a tumultuous journey that included enduring a toxic marriage, battling breast cancer, and grappling with a staggering reliance on fourteen prescription medications, I found myself teetering on the precipice of despair again. It was then that I encountered a mentor whose impact on my life was nothing short of transformative. With boundless empathy and a reservoir of wisdom, she became my beacon of hope, guiding me through the labyrinth of fear, overwhelming emotions, and the suffocating weight of unworthiness.

Through her steadfast support, I learned to peel away the layers of doubt that had taken root in my soul. Together, we uncovered the reservoirs of strength and resilience that had long lain dormant within me. With her guidance, I discovered the power to recognize and honor my own worth, acknowledging the incredible courage it took to emerge from the crucible of adversity. As I stepped into the realm of spiritual awakening, she provided a steady hand, helping me navigate this new landscape with grace and assurance. Through her profound influence, I not only survived but emerged radiant and whole, enveloped in a deep, abiding self-love that can only be described as divine.

Whenever you find yourself at a crossroads, remember this: let your heart be your guide. Take a moment, close your eyes, and breathe in the calm. Trust in your instincts, for they've led you this far, and they won't let you down. You've got this. Believe in yourself, and let your heart's wisdom light your path. Keep moving forward with confidence.

Thanks to these big pivotal moments in my life, like breast cancer, fibromyalgia, and the experience of an unhealthy relationship, I now live with purpose, and I love every second of my life. Having cancer has allowed me to see the inner beauty in all the people around me. It has brought me from living a pessimistic lifestyle to one of optimism, where I am in touch with my higher self and my intuition. I am torn because I wish I didn't have to deal with breast cancer, but at the same time I am grateful for the perspective it has given me, and this is what I share with those around me. My mess has given me new eyes to see. New eyes to share with others.

The experience with breast cancer was only the catalyst that allowed me to step into my authentic self, which has changed my life forever. I have allowed it to change me for the better. I am a warrior, not because of the battles I've won, but because I chose to rise and embrace the fullness of life despite the scars. I am a mother, a beacon of love and resilience for my children. I am a survivor, a testament to the indomitable spirit that resides within us all.

Through my own experiences with dis-ease, cancer, codependency, and unworthiness, I've come to understand the profound impact a mentor can have on someone struggling with self-love and feelings of unworthiness. In my role as a self-love advocate and mindfulness mentor, I draw upon these experiences to offer transformative support to clients of all ages, tending to their mind, body, soul, and spirit in meaningful ways.

In the realm of the mind, I provide a safe space to challenge negative thought patterns and replace them with affirmations that affirm self-worth. Together, we work on reshaping limiting beliefs and nurturing a positive and empowering mindset. Setting realistic and achievable goals is another crucial aspect. I guide individuals towards a sense of purpose and accomplishment, offering gentle accountability to ensure progress. For the body, I emphasize the importance of self-care practices, including exercise, nutrition, and sleep. My guidance aims to help clients create a balanced and sustainable lifestyle that supports their physical health. Techniques like mindfulness, meditation, and relaxation exercises are introduced to manage stress and promote overall well-being, positively impacting physical health. I also encourage body positivity and acceptance, fostering self-compassion towards one's physical appearance.

In matters of the soul, I facilitate a deep dive into values, passions, and desires, aiding individuals in reconnecting with their authentic selves. This process often leads to a renewed sense of purpose and fulfillment. Additionally, I create a supportive environment for emotional expression and healing, a crucial step toward inner peace.

For those who are open to embracing the holistic journey of mind, body, soul, and spirit, I provide steadfast support in the exploration of spirituality. This may encompass transformative practices such as meditation, mindfulness, and immersing oneself in the embrace of nature, all aimed at nurturing a profound connection to a higher existence that transcends individuality. I also offer guidance in the cultivation of mindfulness techniques and the utilization of tools for optimizing executive functioning. This empowers clients to be fully immersed in the richness of each day, resulting in a more profound spiritual connection and an enhanced regard for the exquisite beauty that resides within the present moment.

In essence, my approach to personal growth encompasses a comprehensive understanding of the mind, body, soul, and spirit. With my steadfast guidance, unwavering support, and tailor-made strategies, I empower individuals to reclaim their inherent sense of worthiness and embrace self-love. This transformative journey toward self-discovery and acceptance lays the groundwork for a life that radiates balance, fulfillment, and a profound sense of empowerment.

ABOUT THE AUTHOR

Meet Lynda—a special education teacher, mindfulness and spiritual mentor, and self-love advocate with a zest for life! Juggling roles and fueled by a passion for teaching and storytelling, she dreams big to travel the world and is aspiring to be a global speaker.

Drawing from her background in special education and experiences overcoming health challenges, Lynda combines mindfulness, holistic approaches, and lunar wisdom to craft personalized journeys. Her mission? Empowerment. She guides you through the transformative power of mindfulness, offering fresh perspectives for inner peace between both realms. Together, you embark on a journey of self-discovery and worthiness, embracing a unique path to fulfillment.

From her day job as a Special Education teacher to her business Optimystical Wellness, she finds fulfillment, impacting lives through education, mentoring, and genuine connections. For Lynda, it's not just a job; it's a heartfelt mission to inspire and make a positive impact on every life she touches.

Facebook: https://www.facebook.com/OptimysticalWitch?mibextid=9R9pXO
Instagram: https://instagram.com/the_optimystical_witch?igshid=NzZlODBkYWE4Ng%3D%3D&utm_source=qr
Linktree: https://linktr.ee/lyndabarrus

DARCI ALEXANDER

What Grief Taught Me - What I Thought Was Devastation Became Life Into My Being!

I have faced two extreme kinds of loss, which made for a very difficult five-year period for me.

I had a 37-year marriage and five kids with someone who was more drawn to men, living a secret life of two extreme opposites: one being a very strict religious bible teacher and the other being gay. Instead of being honest and integrating the two, he wanted to keep them separate.

The day that this whole truth was discovered, I thought my life was over! I was utterly devastated! I thought to myself, couldn't he have at least been honest and sooner so that I didn't feel so old having to start over? I was 56 and wanted a life partner for my golden years!

I put myself in counseling right away, and for a whole year I devoted myself to learning about myself and this situation.

After that important year, I gave a Tai Chi instructor certification training at a large hotel in San Diego and was asked why I was staying there by a man named

Richard. When I asked him why he was there, he told me that he was speaking at the World Convention for Codependents Anonymous.

It felt like a set-up from the Universe for me to be open to this answer. It might have scared me off—I sure didn't need a codependent in my life after all I've been through! However, my best friend from childhood had recently told me how this very program had helped her in so many areas of her life after searching for answers for so long.

I then told this man, Richard, "Well, maybe I'm codependent," and proceeded to tell him what happened in my marriage. It was freeing, as I hadn't talked about it to hardly anyone for that whole year while in counseling.

All those married years, I knew deep within my being that something wasn't right, and I took it personally, like I just didn't measure up somehow, that I wasn't quite enough, that something was wrong with me. So, on the one hand, it was nice to know that it was just the fact that I wasn't a man, and on the other hand, I had a lot of healing to do. My ex and I are friends to this day, and I am a happier person now.

Richard and I became friends, and I thought he was too good to be true. After being deceived for so long in my 37-year marriage, I watched Richard like a hawk for a whole year before we started dating. I wasn't trying to impress him in the least. I remember even sending him a photo of me with my little grandsons, with my tongue sticking out. It was not flattering, but he shared how much he loved my sending that photo! My advice in dating and in life is to definitely be unapologetically just who you are! Then your soul mate and tribe can find you. They will not only accept you but also cheer you on! I have learned that if you have to convince someone of your value, impress them, or change something about yourself, then it isn't worth the trouble. It will end up coming out that you aren't the right fit for them. The same goes for you. If you think they need to change something about themselves, don't count on that ever happening. You are the only person you have influence over. Everyone deserves to be someone's chocolate cake, and everyone deserves to have someone be their chocolate cake as well. It goes both ways.

Because of cancer, I only got nine wonderful months to be with this amazing man in partnership. Richard loved the fact that I was a girl and said that he waited for me, his soul mate, for 10 years! We were engaged to be married and lived many years-worth of *fully living* in that short time.

He showed me what it was like to be truly loved for who I am. How amazing it is to feel that! He introduced me to so many wonderful things, including how to live life to the fullest. He lived as if each day was his *last* (to savor and appreciate), and each day as if it were his *first,* (with awe and wonder).

Then, he was taken from me at the onset of Covid.

I was so crushed and in shock. How could God answer my prayer, giving me the desires of my heart, and then change his mind?! How cruel that he didn't take me with him. I felt more depressed than when my husband was caught living a double life. I didn't want to live without Richard. I remember being in the bathtub, crying my heart out, and calling out for him to come and take me. I wouldn't commit suicide because of my youngest daughter, who was a new registered nurse working in the hospital during Covid. It was extremely difficult for her as a young RN in the healing arts to have to witness so much death and to have to take someone off life support and say goodbye for the loved ones who weren't allowed to be there. When I lost Richard, she mentioned that I better be very careful, because she wasn't ready to lose me! I took that very seriously, but if God or Richard wanted to come and get me well, that was a different story.

At the end, I remember Richard saying to me, "I want you to love yourself like I love you; I want you to speak to yourself like I spoke to you."

He had written 2 beautiful songs for me. "No One Holds a Candle to You" and "Darci's Sonata". He called me so many wonderful things including "His Cosmic

Reward" and "Joy Personified". He would introduce me as "His Girl" or "His Beloved".

Here are some of the beautiful words that Richard sang or spoke over me from one of his songs. I needed to learn to infuse the spirit of these kind words toward myself.

"*You are the best thing in my life.*
My soul mate, my woman, my lover,
Companion, Confidant, Spirit Weaver. I was so lost in my doubt, now I'm a believer. Beautiful Lady, Kind Woman,
What can I say and do?
It's You that I cherish.
You're the only one for me that is true,
And No one holds a candle to you! You are the woman of my dreams.
So lovely, So thoughtful, Such gentle grace,
I love you; I need you.
I feel your warm embrace.
You are so precious to me and now I can say it!"

When Richard asked me to love myself as he did, I responded, "I don't want to. I can't. I don't know how."

And finally, "Okay, I will."

That final answer has totally changed the trajectory of my life!

It has been the most amazing journey to learn how to do this! My life has transformed, and now I'm truly thankful for each day. I realized that it was God's love for me and the Universe truly having my back that Richard was kept alive long enough for me to learn this new way to live. How kind! I don't believe it was an accident that we were together for nine months either; it was perfect timing for me to gestate for the true birth of myself. I am so very grateful.

I am a physical therapist assistant who specializes in balance and fall prevention. I am a Tai Chi instructor and master trainer for the Tai Chi for Health Institute, so I can train new instructors to teach Tai Chi to help others in their community. Tai Chi has helped me in so many healing and unexpected ways. Tai Chi is an amazing gentle art and exercise in and of itself.

Since the Universe gave me orders from headquarters through Richard to love myself, I realized just how much I was critical and hard on myself. I hated my body shape and what I thought were imperfections. It was more of a feeling than words and my cells were picking up on that loud and clear! I didn't think my self-talk was bad, but after Richard gave me that spiritual assignment, I realized I had been hating my body since childhood. My cells could sense how I felt about it, even if my words were not so terrible. Body shaming can start young. I remember I was told I couldn't take the dance lessons I so wanted because I had "the body of a Taurus" (the bull is my sun sign).

I have now incorporated self-care and empowering visualization that nourishes my body into my Tai Chi teaching and practice. The moves are perfect for it! Filling up those cells with unconditional love and appreciation. Our bodies have deep inner wisdom if we listen, and since Tai Chi is an internal, soft martial art, our focus connects our body, mind, and now, my spirit.

I can give myself the love that I so needed as a child and as a wife. I can supply the love and care that I wasn't given in ways that have been lacking my whole life. I can now have my own back and take care of myself. I took care of my parents beyond what a daughter should have done, as well as my husband. It was a delight taking care of my five children, but it wasn't easy feeling so responsible and alone. I now use Tai Chi as an exercise that not only increases physical balance but also undoes some of that negative body input. I take the time to unconditionally love and appreciate this beautiful body, which does so much for me! Her eyes love to behold all the rich colors in nature and in sunsets. She takes me places and is able to dance through all of her incredible emotions (including the grief after losing Richard). She can dance while listening to music with the sheer joy of celebrating life! She can breathe in the pine-filled air of the mountains or smell fresh coffee brewing in the morning. She can touch the softness of a baby's skin or even her own. She can taste the many flavors of the world. She works hard for me every day with things I don't even have to think about, like digesting that wonderful food or thinking about my heart beating with every breath I take.

The first time I was asked to teach Tai Chi was by a physical therapist who wanted me to teach it in her clinic. I was so shy and repressed that I said no. I went home and thought about it and all the ways it can help people, and I decided right then and there that I would just get over it for the sake of others! It was the best decision I've ever made. It has led to so many good things in my life (including meeting Richard at that hotel).

When the physical therapist and I searched and found Dr. Lam's certification training and programs to be top-notch, I became a certified instructor. Dr. Lam's Tai Chi for Health programs are safe and very effective. They have been medically researched and are backed by science. There have been over 30 research studies done using the Tai Chi for Arthritis program. The wonderful outcomes are reproducible, so it's endorsed by the Center for Disease Control, the National Council on Aging, the Arthritis Foundation and, the Agency on Aging, to name a few.

Loving this work, I am now a master trainer for the Tai Chi for Health Institute and give training workshops on Zoom and in person to individuals and groups to certify instructors in these outstanding programs. I am also offering my free program on YouTube called "Tai Chi for Rejuvenation".

5 Free Classes using the self-love visualization that helped me to heal.
Class 1: Healing the body and soothing the nervous system.
Class 2: Mindfulness and self-care.
Class 3: Stress reduction and flow.
Class 4: Strength and balance.
Class 5: The String of Pearls / Putting it all together.

I realized that having this time set aside for Tai Chi, as well as teaching it, has helped me really connect to my body. It is slow, and I get to savor the focus of sending my body healing love during my focused attention tied to these beautiful movements. I realized how powerful my body is to be able to heal itself by changing my mindset to appreciate what it does and not focus on what is lacking.

Doing Tai Chi in this way floods my cells with unconditional love and appreciation instead of the negative feelings I wasn't even aware of before. It has improved my health beyond what I have ever known. I've always struggled with my health, even as a child, having had rheumatic fever, and as an adult with diseases such as Lyme. Tai Chi has been shown to enhance the immune system, which I so needed. Even when I was suffering from Lyme disease, which made it very painful to walk due to the swelling and Lyme arthritis it caused in my right knee, I was still able to do Tai Chi without it causing any pain. I would have gained so much weight during that time since I wasn't able to do other exercises.

Tai Chi has helped me in so many different ways since I started a regular practice, but with the visualization of care and kindness I've added since Richard's spiritual assignment, it has even cured cancer in my body.

The cancer diagnosis I received two years after Richard passed felt like another attack on my femininity. The reason being the locations of the cancers in my body. Three different cancers invaded me. I medically took care of the two kinds of cancer on the top of my head with Mohs surgery. They were two different types of skin cancer that had gone deep and wide. They were from the intense valley sun. I now have bald patches on the top of my head. My hair was a big part of my femininity, and I can only try to do the best with what I've got. I still have long hair, but I now use scarves creatively and make it part of my own style to cover up the top.

The third type of cancer was literally in my feminine region, and I shared with my doctor that I wanted to wait on treating that one. The huge reason being that I was now choosing life. I had wanted to leave this earth after Richard passed, but after starting to put into practice his asking me to take care of myself for him and talk to myself like he would to me, with so much love, I felt a huge shift take place! I just knew that my body was changing at the cellular level as my thoughts and feelings changed. My doctor and I made a deal that if it spread or got worse while she was monitoring me regularly, I would follow the medical protocol she thought I needed. She got to observe the power of self-love. I got better on my own, and now it's not traceable!

What I've learned from all of this is that everything I do should be self-care, not self-sacrifice (self-abandonment) or denial (betrayal) of what is right for me. Everyone, it seemed, had opinions of what I should do and how I should be. Differing opinions. None of them matched each other either—they were all over the board! Their opinions fit them better than they fit me. I get to choose now, even the people I let into my close circle. I get to sleep or rest when I need it. I get to exercise my body in such a fun way and in a way that I can stay challenged and never get bored. I even get to do that for my work! It's all self-care, even my play, and taking time out in nature, and the kinds of food that I mindfully choose to eat and enjoy. Everything I do now is an act of love and care for this being called me.

You yourself, as much as anybody in the entire universe, deserve your love and affection.

ABOUT THE AUTHOR

Darci Alexander is a Physical Therapist Assistant, Instructor, and Master Trainer for the Tai Chi for Health Institute.

If you would like Darci to certify you to teach Tai Chi, she suggests starting with Dr. Lam's Tai Chi for Rehabilitation (the program she modeled her self-care after). Please email Darci, and she will send you information so you can share with others this fun and healing art! You will start with a self-paced instructor preparation package. After completing that online course, you can schedule an all-day workshop with Darci either on Zoom or in person if you have a group.

Darci resides in California. Tai Chi is her life, and she loves to travel. Her favorite places are in nature, especially the coast and the mountains. She enjoys art, music, and dance. She loves learning new things, but the greatest is making a difference in the lives of others!

Free Tai Chi for Rejuvenation Classes: https://www.youtube.com/@darcialexanderPTA
Tai Chi for Health Institute: https://taichiforhealthinstitute.org/instructors/instructor/?instructor_id=9282
Email address: TaiChiBlessings@gmail.com

MIRIAM VILLEGAS

My Miracle Baby

"Your baby isn't getting enough oxygen anymore. We need to get to her - NOW!"

What did the doctor just tell me? Now? But she is way too early. She is only 27 weeks old.

"We cannot get her now. She's not ready," I replied.

Everything that happened from then on was like an out-of-body experience, like watching a movie.

I got prepped for a C-section because my baby was too little and too weak to be able to be born by natural birth. They brought me into the labor room, sat me on a bed, and a nurse held my hand while they gave me an epidural. I felt that my whole body started to shake. I was cold - extremely cold.

There were so many people around me, I couldn't even count them. I felt the tension in the room. Everyone was rushing, and then all of a sudden, I heard her cry. Thank goodness. That's what I wanted. I remember the doctor saying that if she cries that is already a win.

I heard someone say, "Look at all that hair."

But I didn't see her and then she was already out of the room.

Based on the HELLP syndrome - a rare but life-threatening condition in pregnancy, which caused all that, I was put on medication to prevent a stroke. After 48 hours, when I was taken off that medication, my status improved, and I was allowed to see my baby.

The nurse brought a wheelchair to take me to the NICU. I had never before been in a NICU, nor had I ever heard of it before. I had no clue what to expect. The doors opened and I saw all those incubators standing side by side; there were so many they didn't even seem to end. There were noises everywhere from the monitoring equipment.

They rolled me to a bed and said, "Here's your baby."

My husband helped me stand up from the wheelchair, and when I looked into the incubator, I was shocked. This didn't look anything like a baby that I was used to seeing. This looked like a little alien. That little creature was not chubby like other babies; it was just bones and skin. How is this teeny, tiny baby supposed to survive? How can it even be alive?

Amaia weighed 1lb and 8 ounces (680 grams) when she was born. She had a big mask over her face connected to a big tube. Another tube was coming out of her mouth, and her head was covered by a hat. Her foot was covered by a blood pressure sock. There were just cables and tubes everywhere. She looked so fragile, and I felt so helpless. I collapsed in front of her bed and broke down in tears. I couldn't believe that was my baby.

I thought, "Please God, please help her. Don't take her away from me. Give her strength to get through this."

It took me a while until I calmed down. The nurses assured me that she was okay and just tiny. I was informed that every baby reacts differently to the incubator and that so far, she was doing well and just needed to grow.

After only 3 days I got sent home - alone. Why can all those other moms take their baby home while I have to leave the hospital alone? Why me? Why did I have to go through this?

Every day I was at her bedside. It was like a mental war zone hearing all those machines going off all over the NICU. All those sounds alone were already nerve-wracking, but what was even worse was when the machines were going off because of Amaia. That meant that her heartbeat was not there anymore, and quickly the nurses ran to her and rubbed her chest and back. Beep-beep-beep - finally she started breathing again.

"Don't worry, that's normal for those little ones. They lose their heartbeat sometimes, but it comes right back when you rub them a little".

Amaia lost her heartbeat quite often and knowing that this was "normal" didn't help a bit. Every time I was sitting in front of her bed, praying that she would start breathing again. It was horrible.

One day I asked the doctors if she was going to be normal.

"We cannot guarantee that. Usually all babies born that early have some sort of developmental delay. We cannot tell you what she's going to have, but we also don't want you to be taken by surprise."

This was an answer no mother wanted to hear.

We were already 4 months in the NICU when Amaia developed some white layer on her tongue. The doctors assumed it was thrush, a yeast infection that is pretty common with babies. After trying out 4 different medicines that didn't help, my husband and I agreed it might not be thrush. However, the doctors said we needed to treat it because that might be the reason she wasn't increasing her milk intake. They wanted to give her one more medicine as a last chance, which was an old medicine that was not used anymore. My intuition told me to not let them give her that medicine, but I was emotionally so broken that I couldn't differentiate good from bad anymore.

"The doctors are experts. They know what to do." I told myself.

We agreed to let them proceed. It was a liquid that was applied to her tongue, and it turned her mouth blue. Shortly after, Amaia started shaking all over. She was cold and had a fever at the same time. She cried and cried and cried and was in a miserable state.

"Oh my God, what did we do?"

She didn't stop shaking for a whole day. She would cry even more when we put her down, so me and the nurses took turns to rock her through the night.

The next day we could see the pure meat on her cheeks and tongue. The medicine had burned her mouth and esophagus. It was devastating.

Immediately I wanted to take her to the Children's Hospital so that a specialist could see her. As the hospital didn't help me to make the transition, I called the insurance myself and arranged everything to get her transferred to the Children's Hospital. Shortly after, she was seen by a specialist, and he told me that we needed to place a feeding tube in her tummy so that her mouth and esophagus could heal. Why now, on top of all the other things, do I have to deal with this? I thought if I hadn't been a special needs mom before - now I am one!

I remember how they put her in a stroller to roll her into the surgery room. I couldn't stop feeling guilty for allowing the other hospital to give her that medicine. After 2 days, Amaia was feeling better. I slowly got myself together and remembered all the mindset work I had done.

"What am I doing? Miriam! You know better. Your thoughts create your reality. Do not let outside circumstances decide where you're going. You create your circumstances." Boom! It hit me like lightning.

I said to myself, "I am NOT going to be a special needs mom."

This was the moment my perspective changed. I knew I would do everything within my power to turn this story around. My baby was going to be normal.

After almost 6 months in the NICU, we were allowed to go home with Amaia. I hired all the therapists that I could find. She had developmental therapy, occupational therapy, feeding therapy, physical therapy, and early childhood therapy. Every day I had at least one, if not 2, therapists working with her, and I was working with her myself whenever the therapists were gone.

I told myself, "Miriam, she's a baby. Her subconscious mind is wide open. She will believe whatever you tell her. Think from the end! Treat her like the baby you want her to be."

I wanted my baby to be normal, so I treated her like that. While I was giving her food through her feeding tube, I was telling Amaia how great she'd been eating and that every day she was improving. I didn't know how long it would take me to see results, but I knew that if I just believed in it, God would help me to give her the life I wanted for her.

I had to feed her through the tube every 3 hours and the feeding took one hour, so I only had a 2 hour window where I could leave the house. It was exhausting, as our whole life was determined by her feeding schedule.

One day I thought, "Why not just take her? Treat her like a normal child. I can feed her on the road."

And off we went! We went to the park, on road trips, to the beach, and I just fed her wherever I was. I hooked up the feeding bag on a hook at the backseat handle in the car, and fed her while driving, and on a hook that I added to her stroller, so I could feed her while in the park. I did not let her condition limit our life anymore. Besides that, I told her every day how much she was improving and how well she was eating.

After 1 year, Amaia's feeding therapist gave her some coffee creamer and, to our surprise, she took it. That was the first food she swallowed, and this is how it started. Amaia liked strong flavors, peppermint ice cream, garlic bread, and coffee creamer. This is how we got her to eat.

She didn't like to eat at the table, as this was where the therapist worked with her, and where she felt pressured to eat. The therapist always told me not to give her food anywhere other than at the table, because she might eat better now as she's distracted but it would cause me trouble in the future. My intuition told me otherwise. I realized she liked to chew on food in the car.

One day I got her French fries and started to give them to her in the car, while she was looking out the window enjoying the scenery. Guess what - Amaia started eating French fries; her first solid food. I was over the moon with happiness. As she didn't have a lot of practice, it took her a long time to eat one fry, but I didn't care. What was important to me was that she ate.

I remember there were times when my husband drove us around for 2-3 hours every night, just to feed her one box of French fries. I know it was not what the therapist recommended, but what was important to me was that I got those calories inside of her.

Amaia was developing extremely well and 3 weeks before her 4th birthday she got her feeding tube removed.

She is now 5 years old and is a completely normal child. She goes to a normal school and has no long-term issues. She's the happiest kid I know. The doctors say she's a miracle baby.

And when someone asks her about the scar on her belly, she says, "I have two belly buttons. One is my belly button and the other is my tubie button that saved my life when I was a baby."

My burning desire for a healthy child made my wish come true. Whenever you want something and are willing to do whatever it takes to get there, you might not see instant results, but I guarantee you that, at some point, it will become your reality.

I believed in my daughter. I knew that I was NOT going to be a special needs mom. I created the life I wanted. Now I help other people do the same - to achieve the impossible by empowering them to believe in themselves so they can see their dreams come true as well.

ABOUT THE AUTHOR

Miriam Villegas is a Success and Mindset Coach and Speaker. She was mentored and trained by Bob Proctor, one of the greatest teachers in the world, on the topic of human potential and growth. She helps female entrepreneurs multiply their income by applying powerful mindset techniques so they can live fulfilled, enriched lives by gaining the confidence they need, believing in themselves, breaking through their fears, and aligning their vision with their actions. Miriam is known for her extraordinary ability to empower and motivate others. She has helped countless clients achieve their goals and overcome mental barriers.

In 2023 Miriam was recognized as one of the Top Coaches in Austin, TX. This recognition is a testament to her passion for enabling others to attain greatness. With a track record of success stories, Miriam continues to leave an indelible mark on the world of personal development, guiding individuals toward clarity, purpose, and personal transformation.

Free Manifestation Blueprint for Success: https://bit.ly/ManifestationBlueprintForSuccess
Website: https://yourmagneticmindset.com
Linkedin: https://www.linkedin.com/in/miriamvillegas111/

CINDY MORTON-FERREIRA

The NeuroBusiness Code: Navigating Life's Journey Through The Power Of The Brain

The darkness enveloped my thoughts, and the silence was deafening. And as I slowly opened my eyes, it was the fear I saw in my father's eyes that I then knew something was wrong and I was not okay.

Breathe and keep focused on your breathing. Dad, what happened? His voice was calm; his words were taking hold of me and swarming me with his love to allow me to calm down but, his eyes were telling me a whole other story.

The eyes that had always been a view to his truth—his deepest emotions, his pain, his anger, his pride, his love, and his joy. Today, the story was one of deep fear, of trying to understand and be the strength in our family.

How long had I been in the darkness? What was the darkness? What was the last thought I could remember? Dad, please tell me, what is going on? "Cindy, my love, you are going to be okay."

My mom, dad, and husband were standing over me, and then they rushed me through to the hospital because another darkness appeared, and I was no longer in control. I was scared—that kind of fear that takes you on a roller coaster, and you just can't get hold of that fear to be able to stop yourself from expecting the worst. If they could hear my voice, it was loud and screaming in my mind, "Please don't let me die!"

Again, the silence, the darkness. Where was I now? Again, slowly returning to my surroundings, with glimpses in and out of consciousness, the memories were all confused: an ambulance rushing on a road, a road I had used for many memories over the years, then a tunnel that embraced me and heightened the fear, a noise ringing in my ears; a smell of the cleanliness of my surroundings; a fear of the words of the people rushing around me. In the distance, there were people standing around with an image of a brain—my brain! Who were those men standing and talking to my family? Wait! Before I run into the forest of emotions and share the journey, let me start at the beginning.

I had been married for a full year, and we chose to celebrate with the people who were so integral to our lives—our families. One year of marriage, and I could not keep my eyes open; all I had wanted to do was sleep. Many would have joked that this was the experience of marriage, but then my world changed in that split second, standing in my childhood home, sharing a special celebration with my parents. I had been talking to my mom, and within a moment, my brain had hit the pause button, and I could clearly hear my mom saying, "Cindy, that is not funny. Don't play such a terrible April fool's joke on me."

"Mom, please help me. This is not a joke." but it was just my voice in my head. I was screaming. There were no words coming from my mouth, just this awful sound. It sounded like a wounded dog that was yelping and breathing. Wait, that was my voice. I was scared, and my heart was racing. I did not understand. Then it was black, a darkness I had never experienced, but little did I know that darkness would be part of my world, and I had to learn to embrace what the meaning was for me.

I had been walking behind my mom, being a typical daughter, insisting my opinion was the right one, the words running off my tongue as I jovially teased her, and then suddenly I stopped talking. I was having a seizure and had blocked the doorway so that she was trapped inside the room. I was choking on an apple I had been eating, and then my mom was screaming. Her screams vibrated at a level that my husband heard and came running from outside.

Their recollection of those fearful moments was confusing, but a picture was able to be formed when they shared all the moments together. I had passed out and was not getting air. My husband got my mom past me and told her to phone for help, and then he returned and turned me over to dislodge the apple that was cutting off my oxygen. He resuscitated me, picked me up, and laid me on the bed. I'm not sure about the moments that came or how the events transpired, but I know that my dad rushed home. They had spoken to the doctors, and they tried to calm my mom.

Then it happened again—another pause. We were at the local little hospital, where they told my family that they did not have the right equipment. I was rushed to another hospital, and all I recall were the sirens.

Again, there was a calm darkness and just me and my thoughts. Was I dead? Hang on! I returned slowly from a moment of peacefulness, and there was my family, my husband, my dad and mom, and some doctors.

There were words said, but it sounded like it was spoken in the distance, and they were talking about someone else. I had a brain tumour that had been growing on the left frontal lobe and was aggressive. It needed to be removed, but because of all the trauma my body had been through, I needed to recover before they could do the operation. They would need to keep me sedated for a better recovery.

My husband waivered, lowered his head, and sat down. My mom cried, and my dad silently stood there, looking between myself and my mom. Then I heard it all again: Cindy, you have a brain tumour on the left frontal lobe of your brain, and it needs to be removed. We will have it tested once it is out to see if it is cancerous and what treatment you will need afterwards.

Do I remember the tears? Were they mine? Were they my parents' tears or my husband's? Was there a sound of surrender to that moment that was going to change all our lives, or was it just a pause, a pause for the moment my world changed completely? The shock had come so silently. Oh yes, there were signs, but without that pause of the brain being activated, could any of those signs have influenced arriving at this point without me passing into the darkness? And the answer is always a resounding no. If only we had known what to look for.

Wait! How are you going to remove the tumour from my brain? What does this mean? All the questions were running through my head. My blood pressure was going higher and higher. The nurses warned me to stay calm. Another needle, and sleep returned.

Breathe Cindy, you have not come this far to have this be your end. I was not even thirty yet. How had this happened?

I was brought back out of the darkness and able to ask my questions. The brain tumour was 5cm by 8cm and needed to be removed, but was situated in a dangerous place on the main artery of the brain. If it was accidentally touched, I would bleed out in seconds. There would be no saving me. It had been growing for approximately eight years and had now become aggressive.

Trusting the specialist was nothing short of miracles aligning and leading me to that exact moment. The neurosurgeon was new to the area and was known to be the best in his field. If he had not chosen to be there, I would have been airlifted to another hospital. But the angels were looking after me, and the timing was on my side.

My main priority for that week was to remain in an induced coma so that my body could recover. Each time I was brought out of the coma, there was my husband, sitting at my bedside, waiting, sharing his nervous laughter, with his beliefs being tested, and willing me to trust that I could do this. The cosmic truth of the situation was that I needed to prepare my estate, say my goodbyes, and prepare for the unknown outcome of this procedure because there were no guarantees of its success.

For me, in a flicker, the week had passed, and I was being prepared for surgery. I had to make peace with the fact that my hair, one of the features that I loved, had to be shaved off.

The social worker had prepared my family for the worst and given me the opportunity to have the hard conversations. The elders of the congregation had come to discuss the way forward. The goodbyes had been said, and then it was that moment of having them wheel me into the theatre.

Unfortunately for my family they had to remain at the hospital for any what-if scenarios where they would need to make decisions on my behalf. I had instructed that I not be given any blood transfusions or put on any life-support machines, and that my organs were to be donated. We prayed together, and I bravely took the stance of my father, with my eyes not hiding my fear, but my voice saying, "Don't worry, I will be back, and I will be myself." I don't know if my family saw or felt the fear, but I was captivated by all the emotions and the uncertainty of whether I could or would get through this.

The nine and a half hours of my surgery felt like nine minutes to me, but to my husband, it felt like nine days. My family sat waiting while the amazing surgical team performed the miraculous operation. I had had my skin and my skull cut open and the foreign being removed—the tumour—that I had named LIFE, because life happens no matter what your plans or intentions are.

I was woken up in the ICU, where the machine sounds were a sign that I was still alive but unable to communicate; my subconscious was asking so many questions. Then my husband said that he was going home for the first time since our arrival at the hospital so that he could have a good night's sleep because the journey to recovery was going to be challenging—for all of us. In my head, I heard myself saying, "Please don't leave me alone." The sounds of the machines monitoring my heart and all the life-saving equipment were putting the fear of God into my soul.

NO. I was screaming, with those terrible, frightening sounds coming from my mouth and my body jerking from the seizure. Another pause, worse than ever before. Please no. Had they not been able to remove the LIFE? Or was this my new norm? Nurses running, another needle, and darkness again; luckily, no more fear.

My road to recovery was filled with new journeys and different lessons, which had to be taught through the changes that were going to be my new norm. My world was now going to be how to cope with the brain hitting the pause button on so many occasions. I was strong enough to be moved from the ICU to a recovery ward, but I had not yet had the courage. Lots of sleep, lots of tests, and many moments of fear—testing medication and then having to test what the medication was doing to the other organs in my body.

To be able to go home, I had to get out of the hospital bed and be wheeled around in a wheelchair. I will never forget the first big adjustment—the moment I had to look at myself in the mirror. I was seated in the wheelchair and had been wheeled into the lift. Who was that person that I had seen in the mirrors of the lift? I felt the dampness of the tears that were rolling down my cheeks. I had to look intensely at the eyes looking back at me. The face was swollen, the hair was gone, and the staples and the scar were a sober reminder that life had changed from here on out.

The original dream would have to be altered, but it was still my life, just not with the LIFE living inside me. The surgery had been successful. Of course, there would be new challenges and lots of learning needed. One of the big lessons was how I saw myself. I used to be this blonde who had danced my whole life, and now, in the mirror, stood this puffy creature who reminded me a little of the childhood

Frankenstein movies. I could choose to wallow in that negative space and ask why. Why me? Why now,? Why, why, why? But I chose to believe that I have the rest of my life to live to the fullest, and even though my world was altered, I know I had to change and that I still have the ability to create fulfilling dreams.

Here lies the twist to this story. A month before I had the first seizure, I had just started my own consulting business, creating opportunities for a world of how best to deal with change and to look at the DNA of organisations and implement ways of helping people manage the culture of how they showed up. The irony was that now I was living all those moments in my own personal life, as I had been tossed into a new reality where I did not know how to control anything or navigate my way around.

I learnt quickly that people show up in their truest form, but this should not influence my truth. Even though my life was different, I had to put all in to ensure that my book, the Cindy version, was going to be filled with thrilling moments and twists and turns, and that with every failure, there was a lesson to be learnt.

My speech had been affected, and I had a stutter. Words escaped me. I had to learn to talk again, and I could hear the changes in my speech. I no longer saw the same person, heard the same voice, or even thought the same thoughts. I had to understand that this was a new me and that life is always changing, and that is the only constant on which you can rely.

I shelved the business for a period, giving myself time to focus on the healing and nurturing of the new me and the voice that I heard back. The road was one of humbleness. I had to find myself and get back into the world. I needed to learn more about the brain and its functions so that I would be able to teach myself new ways of doing things.

Was this what I had wanted? Definitely not, but it was the hand I was dealt, and I had to choose the new pathway. Each new step and being able to listen for moments of my voice and my words reaching my tongue, and the world hearing them as I had intended, were signs that the healing process had started. There were new little challenges that I faced with the intention of ensuring that I was working towards the end game.

I restarted my business but with a new slant. I used the brain functions and equated them to the strategy of a business. I showed how DNA and culture are intertwined, discussing how, when strategy is paused, we investigate and, if required, remove the growths that are causing the pause. Speaking on various platforms, I addressed the audiences on culture and the life of what each individual brings to the sub-cultures.

Shortly after the anniversary of my first year surviving the brain tumour, and even though my speech was a stranger's voice, I delivered a message about the amazing ability leaders have and that even though success may look different, our definition of success needs to be a living organism that grows and is adaptable to the environments that we find ourselves in.

So, when your life is faced with a PAUSE, do you take that moment in or do you go running around to try and make sense of it? Sometimes all that is needed is a strong support system within your beliefs and within your community, and then taking those words that are living in your head and voicing them. Sometimes the journey is going to be filled with many tests and challenges and things that are out of your control: circumstances, people, tumours, cancers, and misalignment of goals. You should hit the pause and align your words to life while also acknowledging that the world has many challenges and that it may take individuals different ways and times to get to an understanding.

We are each on our own journey, and there are places on our road that we can use to learn from and teach from. We need to future-fit our lives, and one way of doing that is by ensuring that we become change-fit. We are going to be faced with experiences that fatigue us and push us out of our comfort zones, but if we take special care to exercise our minds and our thoughts, that will allow us to become change-fit. It is something we have to work towards each day, remembering that whether the change is big or small, we are able to pause, breathe, realign, regroup, and find our path again.

ABOUT THE AUTHOR

Meet Cindy, a dynamic individual whose literary journey has unfolded against the backdrop of a rich and diverse career in the world of consulting. With a wealth of experience amassed over years in business, Cindy brings a unique perspective to the world of literature.

Having honed analytical skills and a keen understanding of human dynamics, Cindy seamlessly weaves real-world insights into the fabric of captivating narratives. From boardrooms to the pages of novels, her storytelling prowess is a testament to the power of combining business acumen with a creative spirit.

Cindy is a storyteller with a passion for bridging the gap between the corporate world and the broader tapestry of human experience. As a consultant-turned-author, Cindy invites readers to embark on a literary journey that aims to entertain, inspire, and shed light on the intricate dance between success, failure, and the countless shades of gray that color our lives.

Website: https://www.cindymortonferreira.com
Website: https://www.dnaatworx.co.za
Linkedin: https://www.linkedin.com/in/cindymortonferreira

JAE WILCOX

The Constant Battle I Win

Looking back, I see two separate versions of my childhood in my head. There was a point in time when I was the youngest. I was the baby of the family, everyone adored me. That point in time, however, appears to me in a fog, clouded by the version of my life I spent raising two little girls. My baby sisters were born in 2013 and immediately became the stars of the show. I blinked and my whole existence changed... but not in the way I imagined. I had eight years of my life to savor the joys of being the baby– the princess. Yet I spent those fleeting years begging for exactly what I got. I didn't see it coming. I realized I had no idea what I had been wishing for.

Over time, I was carefully molded into a "substitute mother" as I think of it. I didn't realize it at the time, but I spent the second half of my childhood being conditioned into adopting the behaviors of a caregiver. My natural empathy was used to turn me from a child into a middle-aged soccer mom. I developed a need to care for the girls, my mom, my brothers, and anyone else I loved, at the expense of having any time to care for myself. But what could I do? I saw my mom in need, and I could do nothing but scramble to take anything I could off of her plate. And in turn, I carried the same weight as my mom did when it came to worrying about the girls. I changed diapers, I prepared food, I played games, I helped them with homework, bedtime rituals, and on, and on, and on. I was their role model. I was no longer their eight-year-old Princess, Cocopuff. I was their mother.

For as long as I can remember my dad has been encapsulated by his work. He was always gone, missed birthdays, school events, and so much more just to take a phone call. A phone call that couldn't ever wait. The issue wasn't that he had to work all the time, the issue was that he WANTED to work 24/7, even if he got opportunities to stay for his family, he wouldn't. Unfortunately, for the first couple years of my life that was the case with my mother's job as well. Being that my two older brothers and I rarely saw our parents, we had a live-in helper (let's call her Grandma). She was hired after Liam was born (the second oldest), and soon became a loved member of the family. Regardless, because it was just us three kids and Grandma she couldn't do it on her own either, so I pitched in. She was in charge of everything around the house, laundry, dishes, cooking, cleaning, and on top of that she also had to take care of us kids. So, usually, I was in charge of the boys, that was easiest. Even though I was the youngest I was constantly making them lunches, making sure they were up for school, and other simple tasks any other little girl could do, right?

Just because my parents weren't around all that much, doesn't mean we didn't still have fun. When my parents weren't working we always seemed happy for at least a short period of time, but eventually they always had to go back to their calls and meetings. Everything always felt more important than us. This was just the beginning. When we found out that my mom was pregnant with the twins, everyone had a different reaction. Ethan (the oldest) was excited but didn't really want to have to do the work that comes with the babies. Liam (the second oldest) immediately crossed his arms and did not want anything to do with the babies, he was very clear about that. I think I was the only one who was excited. Not only was I excited to have sisters I knew a lot of the work would fall on me, and that made me happy. Helping someone out made me happy. Adding more to my plate made me happy. I was always trying to make everyone else happy.

Being a caregiver your whole life is not just a cycle you can break. I have been doing this for almost 19 years now. I am conditioned to put people's needs before my own, and that takes a great deal of time and effort to even begin to unlearn. In this cycle, I wore myself down. I was just a kid who wanted to play a game with her little brothers, but in order to play I had to make them a sandwich. I am just a kid who wanted the company of a sister and instead got two spirit daughters. I am just a kid trying to be a kid, and I was never given the chance. It started innocently, I know that. I was a little girl willing to do anything and everything just to bring a smile to someone's face, to lessen the burdens, and to just help anyone. I truly believe that's how it started, but as people got used to the idea of me always helping out and always being there to make things better, they took it for granted. I felt used. People were taking advantage of me.

Eventually, as I realized this, as I saw the pattern I started to get really depressed. Depressed that my family didn't care enough about me, to try to take care of me. Then, I spiraled. They cared so little about me that they couldn't even realize when I was at my lowest point. One night the dogs ran away. When my dad and I were out in the field searching for them, I was so scared we'd never see them again, my heart started pounding faster, and faster until I couldn't breathe. I fell to the floor and cocooned myself. I curled up into a ball on the grass and my dad couldn't help but scream at me... for having a panic attack. After I repeatedly told him that I couldn't breathe, these were his responses: "If you keep crying we're never gonna find them" "Shut up" "Be quiet" "Stop crying". He definitely didn't care. That was my proof.

If someone needed a right-hand man, it was always me, so I didn't understand why anyone couldn't do that for me. I really didn't think anything of it until well into high school/College. After years of having to be on call 24/7, I got tired. As I got tired and couldn't pick myself up, I realized that although I had given everything to them for my entire life, they would never do the same for me. That fact was proven to me time and time again. When I was at my lowest point, I would hurt myself. I don't like to admit it, but I did. One day when I was arguing with my mom about how she didn't care, I told her I hurt myself, and she screamed back "Show me the scars then". That cut deeper than the knife I used to punish myself for being unhappy. At that point, it felt like she didn't care either. The truth was that she was mad. She was mad that we could be so close, we could share anything with each other, but I couldn't share this. She needed the proof for herself. She was scared. But, that didn't change the fact that that was not the right thing to say at that moment. All I thought was that she didn't care.

Soon after all of this, I knew I had to move out. I had to be on my own and take care of myself for a change. I moved to a college where my first roommates kicked me out because I had a service dog, one roommate was allergic and it caused many complications. There is a lot more to that story, but honestly, it was petty drama that doesn't need to be written about. The next setup was moving into my brother's old college dorm with his ex-best friend. One night that roommate took acid. That same night, I ran into that roommate in the kitchen, he was headed out, but not before he pulled his gun from his hoodie pocket, started laughing and said, "Someone's gonna die tonight". As soon as he left I proceeded to lock myself in my bedroom for the night. When he and his friends came back from the bars I was woken up by the sound of pounding on my door. When I didn't respond, he continued to try and force his way into the room, jamming his shoulder into the door as he and his friends whispered in the hallway. After a few minutes, it got quiet. The last time I went back there, I was escorted by the police. I feel I should add that after my college apartment complex was aware of this situation, they proceeded to tell me that the most they could do was give him a formal warning to remove the firearm from the premises, and that is all. Soon after, I left that college and began to think about what I should do, what would make me happy.

Shortly thereafter, I asked my girlfriend if she wanted to move with me to Texas, where my family lived. To my surprise, she agreed. We renovated an upstairs office space quite literally located in a shed, a spacious shed at that. We lived in Texas for about a year and while we were there we got three cats (to catch the mice in the shed, of course). Recently, we moved to California. We have a quaint studio apartment in the city, and our own lives for once. The freedom and independence you gain from relieving yourself of other people's burdens is unlike any other. I found love in life, love for the hardships, love for the journey. In reality, my responsibility is to make sure I'm happy, healthy, and loved. It's not easy, it's not always happy, but there's still always a glimmer because your life is about you.

The only thing that truly helped me, was realizing that you have to put yourself and your emotions first one hundred percent of the time. I feel like as women, or possibly as humans, we tend to nurture and take care of things that seem hurt or broken. Sometimes doing that though, can make you break yourself when you don't even realize it. This isn't to say that you can't ever help people, or you can't ever take care of others, but there's a difference between giving yourself away vs. giving away what you didn't need for yourself. I had allowed my family to use me until I was drained, and I said nothing about it. They may not have known that they were even doing it, but there came a point in time when I had just as much resentment towards them as I did for me.

I didn't have enough time as a kid to figure out who I was, or what I liked. I was always following someone else, always doing or thinking for someone else. I was so young when I learned to care about people other than myself, that now– I really am still trying to figure it out. I spend every day trying to be a little bit selfish, to try to discover who I am. Being selfish isn't bad all the time, putting yourself and your needs first isn't bad. Sometimes removing yourself from toxic people or people that drain you is for the better. It is a LONG journey. Not only to self-love but to self-care as well. Be a little more selfish. Give yourself some credit. Do things for you. Don't lose yourself like I did.

ABOUT THE AUTHOR

Jae is tenacious. She graduated high school at fifteen years old, then quickly enrolled and attended UC Davis as an Animal Science Major. She learned quickly, however, that a traditional educational path did not support her growth and development and chose instead to return to her entrepreneurial roots.

She started her first company at 13 years old, C. Ainsley, a private-label make-up company. Her second company, B. Hip Designs, was an apparel design company that tapped into her love for animals and focused on unique, one-of-a-kind animal apparel. Her third company, J&K Enterprises, focused on real estate, e-commerce, and retail.

In June 2023, she became a Best-selling Published Author when she published her story in Fearless Female Leaders. She has always been an avid writer, innovator, and creator. She is currently working as the Chief Engagement Officer for Pen Crown Publishing and will soon launch her own publishing company.

Amazon Author Page:
https://www.amazon.com/stores/author/B0C6WZTTSB/about

JENNIFER GRANT

No Ordinary Day

There will never be an ordinary day.

It's something my son said to me when he was very small, before he was pulled under by waves of brain inflammation that towed him away from me. We were sitting on the porch watching the leaves fall from Little Tree, a plush blanket shared across our laps. He squinted at me from under his plastic firefighter hat, very serious: Any of the days can be the beginning or the end.

That's what he said.

And I shivered, pulling him closer and tucking the blanket under our feet so no endings could get in. He was always dropping blurbs of wisdom on me like that. I wish I had written more down, but this was the year I turned forty-five, and I was speeding fast, hopping trains of thought so carelessly. He was always my emergency pull cord.

Today, he sits across from me in a dimly lit waiting room and licks the dimple above his lip twice, nods, and moves his eyebrows up, up, and down. Up, up, and down. Up, up, and down. Then the tic settles into a self-satisfied silence. His fist curls around my phone, partially blocking the speaker as it plays a story from his favorite show about a guy named Bob who likes to build things. A velvet porpoise named Frankless leans against his knee. Frankless is an unusual dolphin—fearless in the face of needles but too frightened of water to even consider the washing machine.

I look up to check the time. We've been here for 45-minutes. My eyes track from the wall clock to a bead of sweat rolling down the outer side of my neighbor's thigh into the invisible pool that turns heat waves into glue. They should turn the air up in here. I test to see if I can peel my own skin off the orange vinyl, and I wonder how many layers of human suffering are now stuck to me.

In the waiting room, there is no beginning and no end. No charge over your future. It's just this stream of uncertainty where your powerlessness ticks and tocks until your mind occupies itself with what-ifs. And worst case. And groceries lists. I need to get honey...

A low keening jolts my attention back to Frankless and his human charge. Frankless isn't paying attention. Instead, he stares blankly at a toddler three seats down who has stopped mid-snot bubble to gape at the strange sound.

The percent is at 16, Mama! That's a bad number.

Sixteen is not a prime number.

And I forgot the charger.

And the next prime doesn't come until thirteen. I've become a bit of an expert on prime numbers. They are a smooth and neat sort of species that can only be divided by themselves and one. The largest prime number has over 24 million digits. The encryption of data is based on prime numbers. So, in a way, prime numbers protect all of us, but particularly so for my son. Way down in the criss-crossed threads of his mind, they perform sacred rituals of preservation. They keep the mad and injurious thoughts at bay. The ones that tell him he will be in jail some day for murder. For my murder, specifically. And that he will die in the bathtub if he stays in it too long. Which could be one of the reasons Frankless hates water so much.

How long does it take to get to 13%?

Too long.

A medium-sized squeal of panic escapes his throat and rises up to stick to the condensation along the metal at the roofline. Any second now, it will be heavy enough to rain down on all of us. Frankless has fallen to the floor and can't get up. Snot Bubble is toddling over to help. If Snot Bubble gets to Frankless first, there is going to be a red-alert germ emergency! People shift in their chairs to get a better look. And someone scoffs that sort of lofty scoff of an adult who has never had to fish a bar of soap out of used toilet water with their bare hands.

The nurse calls us. Finally! And I want to throw my arms around her. Instead, I yelp, "It's here! We're here!" in a voice that is dangerously cheerful. Like those pinatas shaped like fat babies.

This is a pattern interrupt, and sometimes it's all that's needed to avert a full screaming-tear-the-room-apart meltdown. Today was one such day. I cross my fingers inside my pocket and remember to be grateful.

Because we have reached the end of the line. This is THE specialist on PANDAS/PANS. This is doctor number seven, and she will know what to do. She will know how to tuck all of my guts and heart pieces back into my body. And she will know how to get his brain to stop its savage betrayal. She will tell us how to find the ending.

The nurse deposits us deep inside the center of the patient room labyrinth. My son entertains himself by flying his hands through the gaping mouth of the bladeless fan. My hands, though, grip each other to prevent such flight, from which they would probably never return. I distract myself by counting wooden tongue depressors. Actually, shouldn't those have a cover on them? Is that even hygienic?

A doctor comes in—not THE doctor. A doctor. An intern. And she barely glances up from her clipboard as she chirps something about doing the intake, and she trusts that this is alright.

I want to say it is most certainly not alright. We've landed at the Minotaur after three years of wrong turns and dead ends, and I want to speak to the manager. But this is the year I turned 48, and I am still a people pleaser. I slide my hands under me and along the cold metal of the chair legs, giving a squeeze of consent.

1098 days of medical history are efficiently check, check, checked off in less than six minutes. This is not a prime number. And she clips the pen to the side of her board without glancing at my son. Her shoulder tells me my GP will receive the report within 3 days.

I take him by the hand, and together we wind our way in reverse until it's time to go to the GP's office. The report is read. Our access, denied. The diagnosis? Relaxed parenting.

I am alone.

The world contracts into a pinpoint on a scab on the back of my son's hands. He has scrubbed them raw from any germ or molecule of dirt. Thirteen times an hour. That's prime.

The report also goes to his therapist, who recommends a 3-month psychiatric stay in a children's hospital an hour from our home. She tells me not to worry because I'll be allowed to visit him every Saturday afternoon for two hours. She tells me I will be able to check my profoundly anxious seven-year-old into a psych hospital for 90-days where he will stay alone to sample pharmaceutical cocktails until they find the one that makes him follow the rules.

No.

My people-pleasing dissolves out of me into a raging waterfall that threatens to sweep us both into a place we can't come back from. She misses the cue and gives an incredulous pause as I look her gift horse in the mouth. Then she leans across the table and chides me for not recognizing the seriousness of the situation. She's never seen a worse case.

No.

She clucks her tongue, sucking on the air of disbelief, and tells me they will seek guardianship if they deem it to be in the best interest of the child. They. The child.

I stand up to make myself as big as possible because I've heard that's what you're supposed to do when faced with a dangerous predator.

And I decide.

I decide no more. And I yank the emergency pull cord for both of us.

Do you know that the most successful people in the world attribute their accomplishment to the same thing? It's something we wouldn't normally think of. It's the willingness to make rapid decisions. The advice is the same no matter which successful person you interview: decide first, then figure out how. But be very slow to change your mind. See it through to the end.

So, that's it. That's the secret to turning the corner to good things happening. Decide. Then keep on flowing in that direction, taking every failure as feedback on how to adjust the sails.

Decide.

I come back into myself with arms extended and hands clutching the ends of my coat to hold it out. I am a giant and worthy adversary; I am not to be taken lightly. There were some words exchanged with the therapist, but they didn't get stored in my memory bank. What I do recall are the rapid changes in her facial expression:

disgust, shock, defense, and finally something like resignation mixed with fear. That part doesn't make me proud. Just mid-level satisfied.

I leave that office with my son. And we keep walking.

I decide to get a referral to a new pediatrician who works in the same office as the PANDAS/PANS specialist.

I decide to ask him to swab my son's throat for strep, even though he has no symptoms.

Positive.

I decide to ask him to refer us to the specialist, even though her waitlist is now closed.

I decide to help him understand that this is an emergency. And my son has waited too long for help already.

He excuses himself from the exam room and returns with the message that we will be taken into her caseload. A life line is tossed into the rolling sea.

What follows are seven years of treatment that has ended in success. My son is back (for) now. He is currently thriving and happy. It took many trials of medicines and herbal compounds to first kill the hidden infections and then nurture his fragile immune system back into the land of the living.

The prime numbers were the first to go. Then the tics. And the rage. Which has added years back to his quality of life. He doesn't remember much from the time before, but his body does. It protests every demand and every challenge, as if to pre-emptively repel further trauma.

For this reason, we unschool, which is a world people do not understand. There is a frequent intrusive (but welling-meaning?) quizzing of skills that unnerve him and add treads to his resistance. Can you imagine ever asking an adult to recite the times tables or the capitals of all of the provinces of Canada? Instead, he deeply pursues his passions and finds no sense in memorizing facts he can easily access with a whisper to Alexa. I admire that in him - a powerful intention to live with reason over pleasing.

So, is this an ending for PANS? I'm not sure. I have hope, but I remain guarded. There are too many stories of relapse to put all of my eggs in the healed basket.

Today, I work with the moms of children with PANDAS/PANS. I coach them about mindset, about deciding, and about rising to meet the road of an incredible journey. It is with gratitude that I dedicate myself to the work of helping mothers of kids with complex medical needs find a beginning. Because while the diagnosis is not the end, it is a life that looks vastly different from the one we set out to have. There are grieving and intimidating adjustments, but against the sharp stone of the struggle, we shape ourselves into powerful change-makers.

ABOUT THE AUTHOR

Jennifer Grant is the CEO and founder of The Small Moves, a company dedicated to the emotional healing of mothers of children with PANDAS and PANS. She is a coach, writer, entrepreneur, educator, and mother of two.

Jennifer believes in the power of the superconscious to transform and heal the person. As a mindset and transformational coach with NLP Masters certification, she has dedicated her skills to the mothers of children with long-term and complex medical needs. Jennifer specializes in supporting personal breakthroughs via 1:1 and small group coaching.

LinkedIn: https://www.linkedin.com/in/jennifer-g-57082310/
Facebook: https://www.facebook.com/jennifer.grant.946/

KATIE KRETER

The Path Of A Yogini And Healer

Growing up, I was always very sensitive and shy. I often felt like an outcast and different in my early life, as if there was something fundamentally wrong with me. I couldn't understand why until I later discovered this was a common sentiment among adopted children. I was adopted at four days old. My birth mother had me at a young age and decided to give me up as she hadn't even finished high school. There was a lot of fear, shame, anxiety, and guilt for my poor mother at that time while she was carrying me. As I discovered later on, these visceral maternal feelings are felt and transferred onto the baby in utero—unbeknownst to my sweet mother! So, I grew up with a weird sense of shame, as though something was wrong with me and that I did not belong in this world.

My adoptive parents were very loving, attentive, and hard-working. My adoptive mother was also adopted, so she understood the feelings that came with the after-effects of adoption. My older sister was also adopted but from a different family. My adoptive father is a third-generation Japanese-Canadian, born during World War II.

I also discovered from a young age, that I was really sensitive to any sensations in my body. I felt every tension, every block, every minute disturbance in my body to the point it drove me crazy! I felt cursed for having such a sensitive acute awareness of every feeling and every sensation in my body.

I soon discovered I could feel the blocks in other people as well. I could feel others' emotional blocks and even identify them. As an empath and clairsentient, I would see and feel the masks they wore and the armour they put on to cover up their vulnerable emotions, traumas, and pain. Because of this sensitivity, I struggled to be in crowds, as I found it too overwhelming. I sometimes found it uncomfortable interacting with people who were not authentic. I could see through their fears and masks, and my knowing gaze was likely to meet some resistance. I found I was triggered easily as well, being so sensitive to other people's energy. I would often take on the projections of others.

I had struggled with pain in my body since my late teens, especially around my pelvis and hips. I started running around sixteen years old and had several running injuries, multiple stress fractures, and at one point, a particularly bad one in my femur, which prevented me from running for almost seven months.

I was told by a couple of doctors to stop running entirely. I remember when I was in my early twenties, I also had a doctor tell me I should not have kids if I was having so much pain in my pelvis at such a young age. What a statement to make to a woman in her early twenties! Luckily, I was not set on having children and, in a sense, agreed with the doctor. I couldn't imagine having children and going through labor to possibly make my pelvis pain even worse than it already was.

I would often avoid going out at night with my friends as I was just in too much pain. It circled around my body—sometimes my hips, sometimes my shins, sometimes headaches or neck pain. It was debilitating and very frustrating, as it felt like I was missing out on my youth. I felt like I was cursed with a weak, sensitive body.

I grew up with a mother who was very spiritual and was always reading personal development books. I am so grateful for that early exposure, as I picked up one of her books one day by Louis Hay titled 'You Can Heal Your Life,' and it changed my life. Being a Virgo with the typical perfectionist archetype (another common adopted kid trait), the idea of positive self-talk and affirmations was not my normal way of being until this book. It was a revelation that I did not need to beat myself up all day long. I was so hard on myself, as I felt I always needed to be perfect in order to be worthy.

When I was twenty-three, I was inspired to go to Nepal and then to India. I ended up staying in Nepal, teaching English for a month, and then to India for another five months. This trip changed the course of my life.

My intention was to study Buddhism in McLeod Ganj, as I had started to read some Buddhist teachings. When I arrived in late October, I discovered many of the schools were shutting down, as the locals often moved down south where the weather was warmer. I met another traveler who suggested I head to Rishikesh to do some yoga, so off I went.

When I arrived, it was recommended that I go to Agama Yoga School to study with Swami Vikekananda Saraswati. My first yoga class felt like coming home. It felt so natural, even though I had never done yoga, gymnastics, or dance classes growing up. The person next to me turned to me after the class and asked me how many years I had been practicing yoga. I laughed. It just came naturally to me, like I had done it in some other lifetime (or two). There was an immediate familiarity to it for me.

Swami was a yoga master from Romania, an ex-engineer turned yogi. He taught high-level esoteric tantric yoga as well as hatha and kundalini yoga, Gnostic Christianity, Kashmir Shaivism, and Tibetan yoga. He was an encyclopedia of knowledge and likely one of the best storytellers and teachers of the philosophy of yoga I have ever encountered. His talks were so powerful that the audience would be laughing one minute and then crying the next with his moving stories surrounding the yoga teachings. Each evening, he would give a lecture on a different topic, and every night I left feeling completely blown away. My mind was opening to some deeper truths about the Universe and I was hooked.

I had only done yoga for about a week and decided to do Swami's Christmas retreat that he ran every year. We were put on a strict Ohsawa cleanse for those ten days, which was mostly brown rice with the exception of oatmeal. I remember a couple of days into the retreat, I went to Swami and said, "I feel like I am getting the flu, Swami, should I stop?" He simply smiled knowingly, and replied, "Keep going." The flu-like symptoms vanished a day or two later as I kept meditating. It was then that I understood how powerful detoxing is, not only for our bodies but for our minds, which has such a powerful effect on the body. By day six, I felt like I had taken some ecstasy pills as I was at such a natural blissful high.

I stayed over four months doing sometimes four hours of yoga a day. My body started to open up and activate into higher energies, and I was gaining new insights. During a group spiral meditation, I actually fainted and almost hit my head on a post as the energies were so intense! I threw myself into intense meditation, prayer, and cleanses.

I went back to India in 2004 for another six months. During this time, I did my Reiki levels I, II, and III with a fellow yogi I had met prior. I later worked for a month with a Canadian shaman in McLeod Ganj. The shaman helped me with the pelvis pain I was experiencing at the time. This was a pivotal time for me, as it was a deeper introduction to energetic healing.

During one session, he got me to focus on one particular isolated spot around my right hip. When I put my attention there, I had the biggest, deepest, most intense energetic release I had ever experienced in my life. It was a release I didn't even know was possible, it was beyond words. As it released, and as the shaman breathed out the release, I burst out in a deep sobbing cry. The release was a deeply held grief, but it was not my grief. It was too profound and unrecognizable to be mine. It felt like generational ancestral grief related specifically to women throughout history. It opened my eyes to the idea that our bodies hold onto trauma, and not only our own trauma but carried over from generations.

I met another amazing energetic healer in India, who one day met me on the streets in Shimla and sat me down to read my palm and do my astrology chart. He was incredibly insightful. He even sensed that my stomach was bothering me which it was at that time. I suspected I had a mild parasite that was making my stomach feel bloated and sore. He held my arm for a few minutes, and I felt a lot of heat coming through his hand. The next morning, my stomach felt amazing, like it had completely emptied! My mind was blown wide open by the energetic healing possibilities.

When I came back to Canada, I felt called to go to Mount Shasta, California, after reading a book by a man who lived there. When my dad and I were sitting in a coffee shop one morning, I asked my dad if he could drive me to California. He said yes, and we almost immediately packed our bags and left that day. We had a wonderful trip, and eventually he dropped me off at the KOA campsite in Mount Shasta, and then he drove back home by himself.

The next day, I was hitchhiking up to Mount Shasta to go for my first hike on the mountain. An older gentleman pulled over to pick me up. When I got in the car, he immediately said, "I normally don't pick people up hitchhiking, but I was guided to stop for you." This man called himself Allisone. He was a retired PhD psychotherapist who later became a spiritual hypnotherapist. He was very wise, and he mentored me for many years. I would stay with him almost every summer until he passed. He felt like a grandfather to me, and we were so connected. He inspired me to do my certification in counseling hypnotherapy during that time.

In the summer of 2005, I started dating a man I had known through mutual friends. We quickly fell head over heels for each other, so much so that we decided to throw caution to the wind and get married after only three months of dating. Sadly, little did I know, this man was going through a dark time in his life, and he suddenly hit rock bottom despite our newly held love and marriage. He attempted suicide about ten days after our marriage, in the morning, after an odd misunderstanding we had the night before. It was triggered by a benign comment I had made that he took offense to, but it was enough to throw him over the edge. I decided to spend the night at my mom's to give us space and woke up to the phone call from his mother at the hospital, who had saved his life.

I immediately took on the guilt of the happenings from the night before. It was an incredibly traumatic experience for everyone close to him. My new husband was in such a bad mental and emotional space, and there was quite a bit of blame placed on me. Or so it felt at the time.

I still remember his words one day, shortly after I took him for a hike to help him recover. He said to me, "Anyone else would have done a better job looking after me than you have, Katie." I was devastated. There was hardly anything I could do or say at the time to make things better.

He did seek some help from a counselor who refused to see us together despite my request for him to hear my perspective. The counselor had perceived me in a bad light and also accused me of pressuring the marriage. This was the day I decided not to be a counselor and to be a physiotherapist instead, as I realized how much damage a poor counselor could cause given only one side of a story, and from a man who had just attempted suicide.

Shortly after his suicide attempt, I got quite sick, to the point where I was bedridden. The doctors and naturopaths suspected I had endometriosis as it was worse around my menstrual cycle. I had to quit school and work. My husband was not able to support me emotionally at this time, as he was recovering from his trauma (as was I), and eventually we parted ways.

At this time, I was loaded up on painkillers every day, taking around twelve Advil a day during my period just to get through it. I would spend most days in bed or in the bathtub. The bath and heating pad were my only saving grace. I even recall one day jumping out of my friend's car as I started vomiting. I had doctors tell me it was all in my head and that I was simply depressed. It was incredibly frustrating and discouraging. Even my family thought I was just being overly dramatic and couldn't really relate to the pain I was in.

My lovely friend took care of me at his house. I am forever grateful to him for helping me and supporting me during one of my darkest times. He was one of the only people who believed me. It felt like I was never going to escape this reality and that I would be bedridden and in chronic pain forever, keeping my life on permanent hold.

I eventually got in to see a gynecologist who performed exploratory laparoscopic surgery. The surgeon did find some adhesions which he lysised and suspected were due to an ectopic pregnancy. Much to my dismay, my pain in that area did not resolve after surgery. I was very discouraged and felt hopeless that my life would simply be lived in chronic pain.

Around this time, I started to tune into the pain I was feeling in my pelvis to try to understand it. I suddenly realized part of the pain was guilt—the guilt I had taken on with my ex-husband's suicide attempt. I slowly started to unwind this guilt knowing that his reactions were simply a result of his state of mind at the time. Things began to shift in my body.

Through synchronicity, I met my first physiotherapist mentor who was training with an amazing medical chi-gong master. Within a few sessions with him, my pelvis pain was gone. I did not understand how he did it, only to know he had mastered energetic healing. At one point, he was working on my neck and I felt a release around my ovary! How is that even possible? He continued a couple of sessions working directly over my ovary, and eventually the pain simply disappeared. It was astonishing—the true power of energetic healing.

With the help of my physio mentor, she relieved the rest of my hip pain caused by running with dry needling and encouraged me to become a physiotherapist. I finished my bachelor's degree in psychology and eventually did my master's degree in physical therapy to ground myself deeper in the knowledge of the human body, with the goal of also doing dry needling.

Despite several doctors telling me throughout my life that I should stop running, I continue to run and hike today, almost daily. I have completed several trail half-marathons and aim to keep going.

My second race was a high-altitude trail race deep in the Indian Himalayas a few hours outside Leh, Ladakh. The race was at 10,000 feet. I came in first out of the women, and second overall. The male winner and I enjoyed a cup of chai while we waited about twenty minutes for the third-place racer. I was over the moon with pride!

Every time I race, I am reminded of the power of the mind and of the body and when the two are joined, one can push outside normal comfort levels. It is such a good reminder, in other aspects of life, that we need to focus with strong determination in order to achieve our goals. And when it gets hard, we just need to dig our heels in a little harder and keep going. Running continues to teach me resilience and discipline.

I now work at an incredible physiotherapy clinic in North Vancouver, BC, Canada, over the last six years and have worked for a total of eleven years as a physiotherapist. I have been mentored by exceptional physiotherapists, osteopaths and other healers which has allowed me to successfully treat many clients over the years. I continue to deepen my practice and expand my healing capacity.

I have recently embarked on a new exciting journey in Akashic facilitation, deepening my channeling ability and attuning my capacity to attune to and channel higher frequencies. It is a lifetime pursuit, which I am excited to embark on and have started to awaken some deeper new intuitive powers.

My vision now is to help more women online and deepen my in-person sessions, specifically with women who suffer from chronic pain. To guide them with a combination of all the techniques I have learned, especially with a deeper understanding of energy healing, as my life experiences have shown me that the deepest healing is energetic in nature.

My mission in life is to be a clear mirror of embodied Presence. To be a clear channel, so that others can easily recall their own deeper truth just by being with me. The path of a yogini and healer.

ABOUT THE AUTHOR

Katie Kreter (nickname Katie Kay) is a holistic physiotherapist, empath, yoga therapist, counseling hypnotherapist, energetic healer, and Akashic facilitator.

Katie began her journey over 20 years ago, traveling through India and Nepal, studying high-level esoteric tantric yoga, and working with shamans and energetic healers. Upon her return to Canada, she did her yoga teacher training, studied CranioSacral Therapy® and continued her training in counseling hypnotherapy.

After finishing her undergrad degree in psychology, she completed a master's degree in physical therapy. With a passion for blending Eastern and Western medicine, she continued her training in anatomical acupuncture, dry needling and manipulative therapy, and osteopathic manual therapy.

With a keen interest in neuroplasticity and quantum physics, she combines science with her intuitive gifts as a clairsentient. Katie is also an Akashic facilitator, providing soul guidance for others on their healing journey and activating their deeper energetic healing codes.

Website: https://www.iamkatiekay.ca
Linkedin: https://www.linkedin.com/in/iamkatiekay/
Facebook: https://www.facebook.com/healwithkatiekay

MARIA VICTORIA CABALU

My Journey To Self-Love And Empowerment

"*What lies behind us and what lies before us are tiny matters compared to what lies within us,*" by Ralph Waldo Emerson. This realization was the beginning of my transformative journey.

Maria Victoria Cabalu here–a coach, speaker, host, and author. But beyond these titles, I am an explorer on the path of self-love and self-care, a loving wife and devoted mother, and a survivor of self-limiting beliefs.

As I reflect on my journey, my pivotal moment was when an injury to my right leg left me in so much pain that I stopped working as a nurse. I embarked on a path of self-reflection to shift my thinking from putting myself last to putting myself first on the list of priorities.

There was this faint calling from within to show up, but I brushed it off and settled. I've always felt I was meant for more, with this burning desire to really make a difference. Unfortunately, I didn't know any different until I worked on myself and changed from being unhappy and discontent to harnessing the power from within to show up and serve others.

My Childhood

When my parents moved to Canada, they left my brother and me behind in the Philippines. Both sides wanted only one of us. I remember that day distinctly. They were trying to pull us apart as we held on to each other tightly. My brother was crying and screaming, and I was determined not to let go. I felt powerless, and I pleaded with them to stop. As we were being pulled in opposite directions, I tried wrapping my arms around him even more, but to no avail. We struggled to keep together and as we lost our grip, we both cried hysterically.

I still remember his face drenched in tears with his outstretched arms as he tried desperately to reach for me as they took him. I tried to free myself to get to him, but I couldn't. Then he was gone. My heart sank. I blamed myself for letting them take him, and I was upset for not being big enough or strong enough. The pain was unbearable. I was desperate for my parents to bring him back and make things better. But they didn't come. I felt alone, helpless, and betrayed. The big walking doll they sent as a gift on my birthday couldn't fill the void and heartbreak that their absence left.

After about a year, we were reunited with our parents. This incident changed the way I raised my boys. I said I love you frequently and gave them hugs. I was loving and cautious, but fierce! I had a strong aversion to injustice, and I would speak my mind like a lawyer.

As I reflect on this, I realize that time with family and letting them know how you feel should be a top priority. Moments with people we love are limited. We don't have an infinite number of tomorrows. It makes sense to act with urgency, especially when it comes to matters of the heart. I encourage you not to wait. "Say it loud, say it clear," as the song *In the Living Years* goes. Take the opportunity now while you still can!

The Visible Scar

Living in Canada, I recall the constant gatherings. At about age 6, my mom's sharp pinch to my thigh left more than just a physical mark. I kept seeing this image of me sitting with this wig on my head and a frown on my face. One of my mom's friends bought this cute bob-cut wig and they all wanted to see how it looked on me. I didn't want to put the wig on, but when I complained, she gave me this angry look after pinching me, so I complied.

Yes, I received compliments, but the picture with that big frown on my face tells a different story. I can see why it took me so long to show up. While the scar on my thigh faded, I dealt with an internal scar that was visible to no one but me. This would play like a broken record each time I wanted to try new things, and it's one of the memories that limited me from showing up. We are genetically encoded for survival, and survive I did to avoid pain—but never flourish.

Be Happy Like Mr. Professor

In grade 1, I walked for about 45 minutes to get to school, so naturally, I was happy to hear that we were moving closer. I was excited! The school was now just down the street. When we moved into the neighborhood, I noticed the children who were playing outside would echo his name, "Hi Mr. Professor," as he passed by. He was a retired teacher, and he would come around with his bright, radiating energy to ask how we were, laughing and telling jokes.

Then one day we didn't see him. As the days passed, we wondered what had happened. Finally, a lady came out of his yard, and we asked about him. Sadly, she said Mr. Professor had passed away. Just like that, my world turned upside down. You see, for me, he was my source of inspiration. I was happy because he was happy. He had this beaming glow, and it felt good to be infused with that energy. Now, I would no longer hear his good morning, how are you, or see his infectious smile. I thought how unfair it was; he didn't deserve to die. There was this energy about him that I longed for and gravitated towards, and I wanted to be like him. There are people out there who need a Mr. Professor in their lives, and I was one of them.

Perhaps your glow will be the beacon of light that someone needs to see in their darkened world. If you're waiting for a sign, take that leap of faith to step into your power and show up!

My Journey

During the period of adolescence, I continued to feel distant from my mom. From my perspective, while growing up, though she did her best, she struggled to express the love and care that I yearned for. While she's more loving now and we're much closer, I remember moments where her lack of motherly love left me feeling empty and discouraged. Her skepticism towards my personal development efforts often left me questioning my worth. I felt at times that she didn't care about me or how I felt during her bouts of mockery. Likely unintentional, but just the same, it didn't make me feel good. I was her daughter, yet I felt empty. I longed for the connection that my friends had with their moms, going on outings and shopping together. While I was happy for them, I felt something was wrong with me. I felt unloved and emotionally neglected.

On one occasion, I told my mom about a school function for mothers and daughters. Everyone was raving about it, and I couldn't wait to get home to tell her. My excitement quickly turned into regret. She dismissed it like it wasn't important to her; she had no time and didn't want to go. A missed opportunity? Yes, but more importantly, my interpretation was that I didn't matter. My mom is different now, she's thoughtful and very loving and I am very grateful to see this side of her.

My Turning Point

I worked as a nurse for 30 years until an injury to my right leg changed everything. First, it was a ligament tear to my ankle, which didn't stop me from working. Shifting my path didn't sink in until my son said, "You need to stop and heal

Mom!" The command in his voice shook something within me and ignited a flicker of self-awareness.

During a night shift, I felt a snap in my right groin area as I attempted to turn and walk. I'll never forget the excruciating pain. "An adductor strain," my doctor said. As the day unfolded, the pain increased, which affected my good leg. I was done. This was the pivotal moment I shifted my focus inward to heal outward. I delved into the past, unearthing painful memories, and studied ways to heal and care for myself.

My Transformation

From the beginnings of a very troubling childhood filled with self-doubt and insecurities, I emerged as a coach and host of Unleash Your Inner Power summits, finding my calling in nurturing resilience in others.

My life is a testament to the undying spirit within us all—a journey from the ashes of doubt to a place of strength and empowerment.

It was during those times of recovery that I began to truly listen to the whispers of my heart, becoming more aware and in tune with my inner knowing. The injury, while physically confining, truly liberated me.

I attended workshops, read voraciously, and sought mentorship. It was my quest for healing, understanding, and, ultimately, for a solution to the emptiness I felt. There were moments of doubt, of backsliding into old patterns of thought, and it wasn't easy. But with each setback, I found new strength to move forward.

Inner Strength and Freedom

The results, once I began implementing different modalities, were profound. I felt a renewed sense of purpose and confidence. I was no longer the nurse who put everyone else's needs above her own. Instead, I became a woman who valued her own worth and was ready to share her gifts with the world.

Life now is a stark contrast to what it once was. I wake up each day with gratitude and excitement for the possibilities that lie ahead. My relationships, especially with my family, have deepened. I've learned to express love and receive it in ways I never knew were possible. My work as a coach allows me to empower others and help them discover their own paths to healing and fulfillment.

Helping others wasn't a conscious decision; it was a natural progression of my journey. Seeing the transformation in my life, I felt a deep desire to share these insights. Witnessing others break free from their limitations and start living their dreams has been one of the most rewarding experiences of my life.

The Power to Change is Within You: Take Action!

In conclusion, the biggest insights and lessons learned on this journey have been about the power of self-belief and the resilience of the human spirit. My story is a testament to the fact that it's never too late to change your life, to heal from your past, and to create a future filled with joy and purpose.

As I share my story, it is my intention that it serves as a beacon of hope and inspiration for others in that if someone like me with such a troubling past can make it through and show up, then you definitely can too! This journey has taught me that our dreams and aspirations are valid at any age and that the pursuit of them is what gives life its true meaning.

Your journey might be different from mine, but the essence remains the same: it's a journey of self-discovery, overcoming obstacles, and realizing your true potential. I encourage you to embark on this journey with an open heart and mind. Remember, the power to change your life lies within you. You have the strength, the courage, and the resilience to overcome any adversity.

Let my story be a reminder that every step, no matter how small, is a step towards a better, more fulfilling life. "Your life does not get better by chance; it gets better by change," says Jim Rohn. I am living proof of this truth. With my Release Rise

Radiate method, you will discover your true self along with the unshakeable truth that the power to move mountains has always been within you.

Remember that time waits for no one. Why wait to embrace the life you deserve? Why delay the joy and fulfillment that could be yours today? Every moment you postpone your journey toward self-discovery and empowerment is a moment lost in the pursuit of your true potential. Take the first step now, and you could find yourself in a far better place much sooner than you ever imagined. Create the life you dream of today. Don't let another year slip by while waiting. Remember to check out my powerful 1-page Momentum Action Planner, a tool designed to keep you on track with your transformation and guide you on the path to a more fulfilling life. Take that step now. Your future self will thank you.

Hugs and love to you!

"It only takes one step, one move, one action to spark the next one, and from there, you build momentum to keep going. Don't stop; keep pushing forward!" - Maria Victoria Cabalu

ABOUT THE AUTHOR

Maria Victoria Cabalu is a coach, speaker, host, and author. She is a devoted mother of four and a loving wife. Her journey toward self-love, self-care, and empowerment was a catalyst to overcoming her limiting beliefs and personal setbacks.

That pivotal moment—an injury to her right leg—forced a shift in direction from a nursing career that spanned 30 years onto a path requiring undeniable courage and confidence toward showing up on a more public scale.

She developed the Release Rise Radiate method to heal, and strengthen in order to pursue her dreams. Maria Victoria's story is a testament to the power of healing, forgiveness, and the courage to follow one's heart, inspiring others to unleash their inner power and to rise above adversity no matter what age.

Claim your free gift - One Page Momentum Action Planner - Designed to keep you on track and guide you on the path to a more fulfilling life.

Free Gift: https://www.mariavictoriacabalu.com
Free Call: https://calendly.com/innerpowerandconfidence/20mincall
Email: ReleaseRiseRadiateCoaching@gmail.com

ROBIN FRICKE

Miracle Girl In Room 5

Guess what? I had a stroke! On April 13th, 2022, I woke up fairly early in the morning. I'm not sure what time it was, but it was still dark, and my husband was at the gym with a friend working out. They would usually go around 6:00, so I think it was probably around 6:00 in the morning. I had gotten up to use the bathroom, and I was very disoriented. I felt as though I was drunk or had severe vertigo, and it also felt like there was this invisible force keeping me from going to the bathroom. I pushed my way to the bathroom, and once I got to the toilet, I sat down. I had drool hanging from my mouth down to the floor. I remember picking up my drool and thinking, Gosh, this looks like an umbilical cord. I was still very much out of it—discombobulated would be the word.

I then got up and fought this invisible force just to get back to my bed. I'm not sure how long I was in bed before I attempted to get up again and go to the bathroom. This time I felt like I had peed in the bed and that I was soaking wet. Again, I found myself pushing my way back to the toilet, fighting this invisible force. I got to the bathroom and sat down on the toilet. I took off all my clothes because I thought I had peed all over myself. I remember picking up my clothes and looking for the wet spots.

All of a sudden, my body started twisting to the left of me, and I remember thinking, Oh my gosh, I don't know what you are, but whatever you are, you're not getting me. I was able to push myself and use the wall as resistance to untwist myself. When I was finally able to get up, I remember trying my hardest to get back to my bed, and once I got there, I remember covering up because I was cold and wet.

My son had come in to ask me if his clothes smelled clean. I remember smelling them and telling him they smelled fine. To me, I was talking normally, but he later told me I was mumbling, and he thought I was dreaming. I think I went to sleep; I am not sure. I woke up, and I remember rolling over to my husband's side of the bed to reach for his angel heart charm. I was able to move my index finger on my right hand—just barely—but I was able to pull that angel heart charm as close as I could to myself without it falling off the nightstand. I was suddenly unable to move, as if I were completely paralyzed.

At this point, one side of my brain was inside a tornado, underwater, drowning. I felt like I was suffocating, and the other side of my brain was me asking for help in a very still, quiet, dark place that made me feel like I was in outer space. I remember not being able to breathe, and it seemed like I would blink, and then there was a very long pause, and then I would blink again, and another very long pause would come. I was at this point not in my mind anymore, maybe as though I was starting to die? I'm not sure.

My husband came home and, thinking that I was still asleep, went ahead and took a shower and did his normal morning routine to get ready for work. As he was getting dressed, he looked over, and all he could see were my eyes, and they were black. He knew then that something was wrong. He came over to me and asked if I was all right. I was not able to speak, and he knew right away that I was having a stroke and said, "Baby, you're having a stroke. We need to go to the hospital now." He then asked, Baby, are you able to walk?" I nodded my head, yes.

My husband said when he tried to help me get out of bed and pulled the covers off me, I pulled them back over myself and was more or less fighting with him to keep them on me. I was being very modest at that point. I have always been a little modest when it comes to being naked in front of anyone.

He said that when he was finally able to get me out of bed and ready to go, I went into the bathroom to brush my teeth and put on eye makeup. He said, "You don't need to do all of that. We need to go." I was able to dress myself. My husband asked me if I was able to write to him about what was happening to me. He found a pen and paper, and I simply wrote: Shit, shit, shit, still, still, still, still! I think the reason I wrote that is because one part of my brain was still, and the other part was in a tornado underwater.

He said, "I can call an ambulance, but I think that will take too long. I think I can get you there faster." And I nodded. As we were driving to the hospital, I remember thinking in my mind, Oh my gosh, I hope we make it, and I pulled down the mirror and saw the right side of my face melting like butter, and my right hand started to curl in. I remember having that feeling of, Oh my gosh, I hope we make it in time. At this point, I no longer had the drunk, vertigo feeling; I was filled with fear.

We got to the hospital, and he rushed me in, and they quickly realized that I was having a stroke. They took the necessary steps and confirmed that I was having a massive stroke. I was transferred by ambulance to another hospital, 25 miles away. For a normal drive, it takes about 30 minutes to get there, but the ambulance got me there in only 10 minutes. I remember the firefighter/EMT telling me that it was okay, that I was going to be okay, and that we were going to make it. At this point, I felt like I was going to sleep, and then waking up, and going to sleep, and then waking up again. But I'm not sure if that was the case.

During all of this, Jesus Christ, three extremely tall angels, an angel by the name of Sarah, my grandmother Addie Nadine, my stepfather Ralph, and the animal kingdom (well, there were a bunch of animals, so I just went ahead and called it the animal kingdom)—were in a circle carrying me. I felt so peaceful and safe. The stillness and calm of them carrying me stabilized my vitals. The hospital couldn't believe that my vitals were perfect, considering I was close to dying.

This feeling of love overtook me, and I fully surrendered and knew that I was going to be okay—either by death or life. I couldn't intellectually say that I was going to be okay and going to live; it wasn't like that at all. It was this feeling that if I die, I'm okay, and if I live, I'm okay.

Once we arrived at the hospital, there was a large team of surgeons and doctors waiting for me. They had to call my husband to get his permission to operate, as I wasn't able to speak. They prepared me with urgency for emergency brain surgery. They took my clothes off, strapped me down, and had to cut my panties off. At this point, I became very aware of what was going on, and I remember feeling so uncomfortable. The sweet nurse said, "Oh, sweetie, I'm sorry, but we have to do this so the surgeon can go through your groin with the apparatus to remove the clots from your brain and artery."

As I watched them remove the clots from my brain, I started to see, hear, and feel my memories of what truly mattered to me. (I wasn't aware of that at the time.) Those memories came in the form of bubbles popping. They were fast, bright, and clear. I could comprehend every memory.

Children were laughing, music was playing, the food smelled delicious, family and friends were dancing and laughing, and there was so much red wine! Yes, even wine! I love wine! There was also water moving, fire crackling, and wind blowing. The sky looked almost like a galaxy with a lot of stars. It was the prettiest mix of pinks, purples, and blues I had ever seen.

Once in the ICU, I was surrounded by nurses, surgeons, doctors, speech therapists, neurologists, and so forth. They asked me so many questions, and it was like they were trying to trick me. (At least that is how I felt anyway.) I guess I didn't know my birthday or that my husband was only 25, and I didn't know who my son was right away. They kept telling me that I was a miracle girl. My nickname was Miracle Girl in Room 5.

You see, almost all of the left side of my brain had died. It miraculously started to come back to life almost fully, kind of like the flower in the movie E.T. I was E.T., and my brain was the flower. Another reason why I was the Miracle Girl in Room 5 is because 95% of stroke victims die at the hospital or are left in a vegetative state. The fact that I was able to talk and function immediately was, in and of itself, a miracle.

I was never alone, and the hospital staff made sure that I knew I was safe and was going to be okay. I had so many visitors and so much support. My son's track coach even came to support my son and husband.

It was a struggle and a challenge, but I was on a mission to show that I was back to normal and could go home. When the sun went down and my husband would have to leave because visiting hours were over and he wasn't allowed to stay the night as I was in the ICU, I would get really scared. I have never been so scared in my life. I was terrified. I started to hallucinate and have panic attacks. I was too scared to fall asleep. I was scared that I was going to have another stroke because they didn't know why I had such a massive stroke. I started to hav neurological symptoms from the brain damage that almost sent me into seizures.

At this point, I can't remember much after that. I was finally home, still very scared—probably more scared. I had been home for only two days when I had two more strokes. We went back to the E.R. They admitted me, gave me a CAT scan, and realized that I had two more strokes.

Those nights in the hospital were one of the scariest moments of my life. I was truly afraid that I was going to die, and I wasn't ready. There is a lot of damage from having a massive stroke. I couldn't read, write, spell, or count. I couldn't see numbers or words in my mind. I couldn't feel anything either. I did physical, occupational, and speech therapy for a whole year. I was fortunate enough to get approved for a hundred sessions through my insurance, and then once those were up, I paid out of pocket because I was determined to get better.

I had lost most of my memories and education. I had just started driving with confidence a month and a half ago. My life was forever changed. My confidence, security, and independence were idle. I was lost, scared, depressed, angry, and at times suicidal. Two things that have helped me get through all of this are knowing that God isn't done with me and that Jesus Christ, the angels, my loved ones, and all the animals carried me back to my life, and I had to Re-Member who I truly am!

Remembering is bringing our "members" or parts of ourselves back together. By remembering who I am, I am bringing back my original connection to my deeper self. I may not remember who I was in the physical realm, but I know and remember the essence of who I am. I am a fighter, a warrior, and a believer whose faith and fire are unwavering. I am light and love! I have a purpose. We all do.

Even today, there is still no true answer in the medical field as to why I had a massive stroke. According to all the tests, numbers, and images, I am considered to be a mystery. I knew I had to take my health and my power back!

My message for you is to live in the present moment, and if you don't know how to, seek guidance. Embrace all of your senses and the beauty nature offers us (24.7). Slow down, see, smell, taste, touch, listen, and feel with full presence.

I lost some of my senses, and I was forced to only be in the moment due to the severe long-term and short-term memory loss. I remember calling my twin brother crying because of how lost I felt being in the moment because I didn't know how. I also felt guilty for not accepting it as the gift that was given to me. I had so many identities: career, motherhood, wifey, education, daughter, sister, friend—oh my! I was trying to remember what I thought made me me. I had done the work to heal, I thought, so why this now?

I don't know the answer right now, and maybe I never will, but I do know not to ever take myself or the people and things that I adore and cherish for granted. I know that I am still meant to do great things, and it's okay that I can't save the world. What I can save are the things that feed my soul. That was proven to me when I was having emergency brain surgery. Everything that brought me great joy and love stayed with me. I re-membered Robin! I am closer than ever to God, Jesus Christ, and my faith. We are never alone!

ABOUT THE AUTHOR

Robin Fricke comes from a military family, which enabled her to travel and experience other cultures and different parts of the world. She lived in the beautiful mountains of Alaska, where she admired the native spiritual healing modalities.

She was a very ill young woman who could not find the answers she needed to heal. When she began her personal healing journey, she knew something miraculous had just taken place. She deepened her exploration of the world's holistic healing traditions and started to understand the healing power we hold within ourselves. She made a promise that once she found the secret to this mysterious illness, she would share it with the world.

Robin is a board-certified holistic health practitioner, CEO, and founder of Root Cause, an online women's holistic health practice and a 12-month personal growth and transformation program, The Goddess Circle.

Website: https://www.robinfricke.com
Facebook Group: https://www.facebook.com/robin.stockdale.5
Email: emotionalroot@gmail.com

ROBYN EYRE-LONG

The Forgiveness Within

It was a very brisk and early morning in the fall when I was gifted to two young adults on an air base in California. It wasn't long after that that my life growing up in Utah began, being raised in a deep-seated religion and structured through military and first responder influences. Childhood during the 1970s and 80s was spent outside in the fresh air, playing with the neighborhood kids, coming in when the streetlights came on, and being a faithful daughter of God by attending all weekly church meetings. I had no complaints, as all my friends were being raised very similarly, and we were all very happy. One of my favorite memories was running through the pathways under the tall, lush pine trees at my Great Aunt's house, communing with the fairies and gleaning wisdom from all varieties of nature.

My teenage years became a little tumultuous when my parents separated and finally divorced, causing me to step more into daily responsibilities to help my mother and younger brother and leave behind the whims and wishes of fairy tales. Those teenage years were full of what to do and what not to do based on church doctrine, my parents' actions and behaviors towards each other, as well as discovering my own direction intermingled with relationships– personal and intimate –through junior high and into college. I always seemed to be dating someone, never left alone for very long, and always looking forward to who would enter my life next.

In college, I explored my sexuality, as many do; however, in private, as this was a main sin with the church, and I did not want to bring shame to myself or my family. After a few encounters with women, the religious guilt kicked in. I became depressed and knew I better start searching for a man who was everything I was taught to marry if I was ever going to come out of this depression and find my bliss in life.

I met my soon-to-be husband while in my junior year of college. He was everything I was supposed to marry: a member of the church with morals and values; he didn't serve a mission but was serving in the military, and he said and did all the right things– at least I told myself he did. Three months after we met, we were engaged and six months later, we were married. I knew, walking down those stairs into a sea of US Marines, that I was not supposed to marry this man, but I was going to stop the lineage of divorce in my family and stand by my commitment to him, to myself, and to the church.

Over the next 13 years, we moved nine times within five states, had two beautiful children, weathered extended separations due to deployments, and I survived three months of being deathly ill after my first child was born. We weren't perfect, but boy, those around us sure thought we were. Every move was "let's start over," and it worked for a few months before going right back into the depression and despair of the cycle of mental and emotional abuse that we were causing within ourselves and to each other.

Within 2 years of my second child being born, the mental and emotional abuse was moving into intimidating physical abuse, and I needed a break. We were living in Minnesota at the time, and I had not been home to Utah and my family for a couple of years. I packed up the kids and told my husband, "Whether we are together or not, I will be back; it is not fair to keep the kids away from you".

The kids and I packed up a few things and traveled the States, stepping firmly into the Salt Lake Valley on June 1, 2009. I was already feeling better being around family; however, I was silently continuing to carry the burden of torturous thoughts and feelings from my marriage that I had been hiding from my family because we were the "perfect temple married couple". Three weeks later, I found myself sitting in a playground at a nearby elementary school overlooking the Salt Lake Valley, and I called my husband and told him I wanted a divorce. This was not a decision I made lightly, but I had a knowing it was the right choice to make. We had a very adult conversation about the cycle of abuse we were living in. We spoke openly and honestly, both owning our parts and knowing it wasn't healthy to continue this way for either of us or the children. I told him I would file for divorce and I would take care of everything, and he agreed.

The very next day, a job offer came in that would allow me to stay at home with the kids–confirmation I had made the right choice. The kids and I enjoyed being with family that summer, spending time at my mother's, at the cabin with my father, and even in Southern Utah with my lifelong best friend. At the beginning of August, we moved into my brother's house. It was the perfect arrangement for both of us, a safe place to live and raise our children, being surrounded and supported by family and friends–a new chapter was opening for us all.

As the kids and I were settling into our new life, with a new home, new school and new job, I began to reflect on my marriage–the places we lived, the people we met, the opportunities we had. We had a good life. I have friends all over the world, and we lived in amazing places because of the military. For this, I would be eternally grateful, and now I could truly see the masks we wore through it all. I also saw how I allowed my health to get out of control, mentally, emotionally, and physically. It was time to truly find myself. I was grateful that the kids' father and I were on the same page and willing to work through the distance until he could get closer, and then, WHAM–a major sucker punch to the gut–I was served with divorce papers declaring his desire for full legal and physical custody, alimony, as well as horrible descriptions of how I was an unfit mother–my world crumbled.

I went into full-blown depression and anxiety about the unknown all while putting on another mask that everything was okay, working full time, being a single mom, and trying not to lose my sense of self with everything that my soon-to-be ex was saying about me. We were all doing the best we could with what we had, as we had only planned to be home for the summer and most of our belongings were still in Minnesota.

We planned to travel to the frozen north in November for the kids to spend Thanksgiving with their father while I packed up all our belongings to move home. Things were so bad between me and their father that I had to have a court order to be "our house" with the kids while he was at work and had to have the police nearby when we would "exchange" kids for everyone's safety. I shut down again mentally and allowed his hurtful and angry words to worm their way into my mind again. I was scared for me and the kids while in Minnesota. The only redeeming light I had was a scheduled mediation to finalize the divorce proceedings, so I thought, and that blew up with him throwing a chair and storming out, wanting a judge to decide the fate of the children's custody instead of their parents. Little did I know, this was a foreshadowing of what was to come for the next 13 years of our lives.

A year later, the divorce was final. I was granted physical custody, and shared legal custody, and awarded more support than I asked for. The kids and I were doing well, and their father had moved to Colorado. I traveled there once a month for work, which allowed for regular visits and a weekend to myself, which I took advantage of when I could. I was grateful for the time the kids got with their father and his family, but not grateful for the continued verbal abuse he chose to direct at me, at the kids, and at whoever would listen. This would continue for many years until I truly started my healing journey.

I began to date and found my attraction was being drawn to women more than men. I was nervous yet excited to explore and trust my feelings, my own knowing, instead of what I had been taught my entire life through church and family beliefs. I "came out" to my family in 2011, some questioned and were concerned, but for the most part supportive and trusting. There was a sense of freedom in choosing who I wanted to be with. Even though my sexuality was shifting, my relationship patterns had not shifted. Awareness became the key as I stepped cautiously into new relationships.

In 2014, I was invited to a "gallery reading" by a friend. I did not know what to expect at this event, and even during the evening, I was unsure of what would transpire. The practitioner was a theta healer and a medium, and she was connecting us to a past loved one with a message. My amazing Great Aunt, who taught me about fairies, was there for me that night in Spirit with a beautiful and healing message that was the catalyst for who I was to become. I began working with this healer monthly, healing the shame and religious guilt as well as truly believing that everything I had been through was divinely orchestrated for me and my children.

In 2016, I connected with a dear friend whom I watched go through a massive transformation over the past year. He introduced me to Reiki, a Japanese healing technique for physical, emotional, mental, and spiritual healing. After one Reiki session, I knew I needed this in my life, and I began my journey to becoming a Reiki Master. The Reiki Master I chose became my mentor, healer, and friend as I journeyed through my Reiki attunements into a journey of self-discovery, ready to share my wisdom and knowledge with others, beginning my Reiki practice later that year.

My passion for healing myself intensified, as did my desire to assist others on their healing journeys. I took course after course, becoming certified in over a dozen different healing modalities. My intuitive and empathic gifts began to bloom like a lotus flower nurtured in the mud, and I was feeling more divinely guided every day. Connecting with others on their own healing journey, I was able to unravel that my misguided intention of stopping divorce in my lineage was actually co-dependency that needed healing. I truly wanted to become the best version of myself, sovereign and authentic in all ways.

One day, I was speaking with a friend about my journey and a recent situation with my ex-husband. She felt the pain that still lived within me and introduced me to the book "The Little Soul and the Sun: A Children's Parable" by Neale Donald Walsch. This book was a gift of love, and it changed my life, my perspective, and my trajectory of healing. It wasn't about what my ex-husband was continuing to say about me; it was about how I perceived it. Through this children's story, I came to realize that he chose to be this way towards me so that my children and I could learn unconditional love, forgiveness, compassion, humility, and so much more.

I dove into forgiveness work, learning that forgiveness doesn't require condoning poor behaviors or even forgetting them. Forgiveness is seeing the situation in a new light, in a different way, from a new perspective. Forgiveness is a transformative process that occurs within us, granting us the freedom to love unconditionally. This love is not contingent on altering the past or predicting the future; it arises when we confront the darkest aspects and declare, "I forgive you, and I love you." It's an act of grace, even when the recipient may not seem deserving, because ultimately, it's a gift we offer to ourselves.

I was finally seeing the light of shifting my perspective to be able to step back and see the bigger picture. We become so pinpointed on the act or the word that we don't–or don't want to–see the full picture. This became my focus, and I wanted to continue my work of forgiveness. To obtain this level of forgiveness and perspective, I had to ascend to a higher level and do the work in the energetic and soulful realms. I was shortly thereafter introduced to Contract Space, or, to some, the Akashic Records.

During my first session of healing in Contract Space, I set my intention to discover what it was that I had a fear of seeing. I witnessed my ex-husband's physical death, and with it, the end of the cycle of abuse and anger toward others. I watched him cross into the light holding the hand of his grandmother, knowing she was going to help him understand this lifetime and how he showed up for me and for our children. I continued to do regular contract healing sessions, each time understanding more of my life purpose and the choices and directions I was to make.

The kids and I continued to thrive, learning from each other and from those who came in and out of our lives. The years passed so quickly: my son had graduated and was away in another state playing junior hockey, and my daughter was enduring the teenage years of junior high school. I had a couple of relationships that lasted a few years but ended the same–taking different paths. I had chosen to raise my children to think for themselves, to trust themselves, and to choose their path, not the path of others or others' expectations, as I had done over the years or that their father continued to do.

Eight months after that first healing session in Contract Space, we became aware of their father's terminal diagnosis of ALS (Lou Gehrig's Disease). Communications were open again, and we planned to visit at the end of June. I was pleased with the communication that was happening and thought we had finally made it past all the anger. The kids and I packed up for a trip to Colorado to see their father and do some college visits in Denver. The closer we got to Pueblo, the more we felt unsettled. The kid's father's mental status had changed again, and because I was accompanying the kids, though I had made no plans to see him or be near him, he packed up and left the state, telling the kids he never wanted to see them again. This was devastating to all of us. Emotions were high, yet there was a sense of knowing this was exactly as it was supposed to be. The kids and I took an extended vacation, seeing the sites of Colorado and bringing closure to an era of our lives that we would not visit again.

The following year, 2020, I opened a healing studio in May, just months after Covid hit the U.S. It became a place of POWERFUL healing in a CALM environment that felt like HOME. My healing business was growing as well as my confidence in my own abilities and gifts. Clients were seeking help with acknowledging repeating patterns in their lives that no longer served them, and I was able to empower them to transform their beliefs. It was a blessing to witness such transformations during sessions.

I continued doing my healing work, feeling the release of the weight of pain, anger, shame, frustration, expectations, obligations, family structures, and ideals that I had been carrying for so long. I was grateful for this journey to be able to stand in my own power and entrust the same to my children.

Just prior to the two-year mark of my ex-husband's diagnosis, he passed away. The kids got to send him a final message, but his thoughts had to be conveyed to them through his wife, as, with this horrible disease, he had lost his ability to speak. As the kids and I discussed the funeral, there were a lot of concerns about the viewing being 10 hours away and the burial being 5 hours away and knowing I was not welcome to attend with them. I asked my son, "No expectations and no obligations, what would you do?" The next day, he came to me and said he chose to stay home and attend college hockey tryouts, and my daughter chose to run my healing fair that weekend. We decided to honor their father in our own way.

I know that this lifetime has afforded me many opportunities to learn and grow, knowing the good with the bad and the light with the dark. I know that it was through my desire to obtain true forgiveness and offer unconditional love to myself and others that I was able to entrust my children to make their own decisions. To stand in their own power and truth. To not waiver in the decision that was best for them.

To be in a place to learn from others, and sometimes be the lesson for others, is truly a place of higher perspective. To live in a space of continuing to choose forgiveness and to send unconditional love to others, of choosing gratitude over pain, has become my beacon, my path, my purpose. This is the gift I extend to my clients: the guidance to learn from their own life experiences, to step back and gain a larger perspective, and to embrace the profound forgiveness within–for self and others. It's the key to liberating ourselves from the past and savoring each present moment with genuine happiness.

ABOUT THE AUTHOR

Robyn, the visionary behind Clear Healings, brings over a decade of experience to her clients as a Transformation and Empowerment Mentor. She's also the creator of the international virtual summit "I Am Something Beautiful" and a featured guest on multiple podcasts.

Beyond her roles as a Reiki Master and Intuitive Healer, she's a Master Hypnotherapist. Her unwavering dedication to healing and personal growth empowers her to guide others on transformative journeys, where she has cultivated expertise in diverse healing techniques.

At the core of Robyn's mentoring philosophy are the values of forgiveness and perspective. She genuinely believes that every individual is inherently worthy and perfect in their unique way, dedicating herself wholeheartedly to helping individuals release their past conditioning, embrace the present, and discover the bliss of each moment.

Website: https://www.clearhealings.com
Facebook: https://www.facebook.com/clearhealings1
Instagram: https://www.instagram.com/clearheaings1

SANET VAN BREDA

Forgiving Yourself - Letting Go Of Shame And Regret

"Set yourself free by letting go of any shame and regret in your beautiful life." Sanet Van Breda

Once upon a time, in a mystical kingdom, on a sombre day by the tumultuous, storm-laden waves of the vast ocean, the black sand extended beneath my feet as far as the eyes could fathom. At the horizon's edge, a magnificent cave adorned with lush greenery served as the captivating culmination of this breathtaking view before me.

With an umbrella clutched as my feeble walking stick, a desperate attempt to catch up with my family unfolded. Ahead, my husband Petrus, my son Dawid, my daughter Estie, my son-in-law Petrus, and my cherished little grandson Zander were visible in the distance, drawing nearer to the enticing cave. The weight of my colossal body became an oppressive force, resisting every step and making each breath a laborious task. I pressed on, my feet sinking into the yielding sand with each staggering stride, a poignant metaphor for the weight I carried—not just in pounds but in the burden of my very existence. The heaviness of my own body mirrored the emotional weight, an unbearable load that seemed to intensify with every beat of my struggling heart.

Shame and regret are powerful emotions that can have a profound impact on our lives. It can haunt us, reminding us of our past failures and shortcomings. It whispers in our ears, replaying our mistakes over and over again, making it difficult to forgive ourselves and let go. Regret, on the other hand, often stems from a sense of missed potential. We look back at opportunities we didn't seize, choices we wish we had made differently, and wonder what could have been.

When we carry a heavy burden, it permeates every aspect of our lives. We may find ourselves stuck in negative patterns of self-talk, constantly berating ourselves for past actions. Our self-esteem and self-worth suffer as we believe we are unworthy of forgiveness or happiness. We may even shy away from new experiences or opportunities, paralyzed by the fear of repeating past mistakes. In this state, we become prisoners of our own self-judgment, unable to fully embrace our true potential.

In that pivotal moment, doubts began to creep into my mind like insidious whispers, questioning why I had chosen this challenging path. The once alluring sand, now a hindrance, made every step feel like an arduous feat. A cascade of self-doubt and self-reproach flooded my thoughts. Why, oh why, did I not foresee the added difficulty this sandy terrain would impose on my already strained journey?

As the struggle persisted, I found myself kicking at my own spirit. Here I was, presented with the extraordinary opportunity to explore enchanting caves and witness nature's erosion masterpiece, yet I couldn't fully embrace it. Instead, my internal dialogue became a relentless critic, insisting that I could conquer this and urging myself to go just a little farther. But with every step, the inner praise I sought was eclipsed by the growing realization that, perhaps, I wasn't physically equipped to reach the cave. The longing for normalcy echoed within me, a plea for relief from the relentless challenges that seemed insurmountable. When, I wondered, would this cease? When could I experience the simplicity of being just normal?

The struggle or our barrier can strain our relationships with others, making it challenging to connect authentically. We may build walls to protect ourselves from vulnerability, fearing that if others truly knew our past, they would reject or judge us. This self-imposed isolation can lead to loneliness and a profound sense of disconnection, further intensifying the emotional weight we carry. Our inability to forgive ourselves can also result in a cycle of negative behaviour, as we unconsciously seek to punish ourselves for our past mistakes, inadvertently harming those around us in the process.

The physical strain exacted a toll beyond measure, pushing me perilously close to the precipice of what felt like an imminent heart attack. Each breath became a laboured gasp, accompanied by waves of excruciating pain that surged through my entire being. Amidst this torment, the haunting image of my precious grandson, Zander, innocently questioning, "Oumie (Afrikaans for Granny), why aren't you in the picture in the cave?" reverberated in my mind.

The anticipated response, "Zandertjie, your Oumie is too fat!" weighed heavily on my conscience. Each utterance of those words intensified the self-loathing that gripped me, my body becoming a vessel of despair.

In that agonizing moment, I found myself questioning, "Why? Why? Why?" It's not for lack of trying, not for a shortage of diets embarked upon throughout my life. The earnest efforts persist, yet the stubborn fat clings to me tenaciously, refusing to relent. The mere contemplation of confessing that my weight had become an insurmountable barrier stirred a profound sense of nausea. Overwhelmed by despair, I crumbled to my knees, a desperate supplication escaping my lips, "Please, God, help me. I can't endure this any longer!"

Desperately staring at the ocean, my tears mingling with the salty breeze, I cried out louder than the roaring waves, my plea echoing against the vast expanse. "God, help my! Ek weet nie meer nie, ek is verlore, ek weet nie hoe om hieruit te kom nie. Red my asseblief!" (God, help me! I don't know anymore, I'm lost, I don't know how to get out of this. Save me, please!). With my tear-streaked face buried in the palms of my hands, I sobbed, feeling as if there might be no tomorrow. In this very moment, I recognized that it was my day of no return. At 54 years old, burdened with this overweight body since the tender age of 12, the weight of despair became too much to bear. "I can't do this anymore."

In that moment of desperate longing, a miracle unfolded, and I found myself cradled in the warmth of God's divine embrace. In that poignant moment, the sun emerged from behind the concealing clouds, casting its warm, golden glow upon the landscape. His intervention wasn't just the gentle touch of the sun on my face; it was a profound experience where His love and grace enveloped not only my face but also radiated through my entire being.

As I bathed in the glow of His divine light, I felt a whisper of reassurance—a tender acknowledgment that it was time to face me—Sanet—embracing every facet of me, flaws and all. Rising from my knees, a renewed determination blossomed within me. The path ahead might have seemed formidable, but a flicker of hope now danced brightly in my heart, propelling me forward. It was more than a journey; it was a divine pat on the back, a loving assurance that I was not alone. Every step I took was guided by the assurance that I was cherished and worthy, and that He would be my constant companion through it all. I was "Walking on Sunshine."

I feel the heartwarming joy as I approach the cave, and my grandson Zander comes running towards me, his face beaming with happiness. "Oumie jy het gekom, Oumie ek soek jou" ("Granny, you came! Granny, I was looking for you!") I scoop him up in my arms, twirling around with him. His laughter is a magical symphony to my ears, causing my heart to beat even more fervently. Little did I know, this precious moment captured in my mind would serve as a powerful anchor, motivating me to stay on course with my plan to reclaim my life.

Envision a life where we rewrite the narrative of our past, present, and future. On a journey of imagination, similar to the sentiments expressed in John Lennon's timeless song "Imagine". In this life, we have the power to truly let go and embrace the freedom that forgiveness brings. For me, this transformative journey commenced with the realization that my weight had become an overwhelming burden. It transcended the desire to fit into smaller clothes or adhere to society's beauty standards; it was a quest to reclaim my health, confidence, and self-worth. Deep within, I recognized my deservingness of a life unburdened by the chains of guilt and shame that had imprisoned me for far too long.

Later in the day, as I stood before the mirror, a revelation unfolded: I saw myself not as a prisoner of my weight but as Sanet, defined by an intrinsic worth beyond the physical. Tenderly, I reached out, tracing the contours of my eyes, nose, and lips. With gratitude, I whispered to God, "Thank you, my beautiful Savior, for caring for me, even in this substantial body." Gazing into my own eyes and acknowledging my weight loss aspirations, I grasped the purpose of my journey.

The answer surfaced effortlessly, adorning my face with a smile. "I want to lose weight to be with my grandson Zander every day." New Zealand's regulations stipulated a working permit for a BMI of 35% or less; shedding the weight became not just a health improvement but a means to savour invaluable moments with Zander. Closing the gap to the mirror, our reflections nearly merging, I posed the question once more, "Yes, Sanet, you want to lose weight to be with your grandson Zander. But why?" The response came swiftly and resolutely. "I want to swing on a swing next to him, run on the beach together, and play with my precious grandson," I exclaimed with unbridled excitement.

With the mirror inches from my face, the third query hung in the air, anticipation building. "Yes, Sanet, you want to lose your weight for Zander to play with him. But why?" Shock echoed in my eyes and heart, tears streaming down my face. The answer struck with unwavering clarity, hitting between the eyes and piercing my chest: "I want to live. I WANT TO LIVE AND NOT DIE! I've discovered a potent motivation: to be with my grandson Zander and play with him." This became my driving force, a daily reminder to stay focused and committed to my Oumie and Zander Plan, my journey, and my life.

I intimately understand the challenges of carrying excess weight, a lifelong companion since childhood. In a journey marked by teasing and self-doubt, adherence to any eating plan felt elusive, often tempting me to surrender. Trapped in a cycle of attempting myriad diets, aspiring to shed weight, only to oscillate like a yo-yo between starting, stopping, and restarting. The road ahead appeared daunting, and I understood that it would demand unwavering dedication and hard work. It was not a quick fix or an overnight solution; it required a complete shift in my lifestyle, eating habits, and mindset.

It was about rewriting my own narrative, envisioning a life where I could replace guilt with self-compassion and shame with pride. This journey was not just about shedding pounds; it was about gaining a profound sense of freedom and embracing a world of possibilities where success, healing, and self-love were not mere dreams but the very essence of my existence. Above all, deep in my heart, I knew I wanted to live. I didn't want to merely exist. I wanted to be 120 years old, witnessing my incredible grandchildren become who they wanted to be and making the world a better place.

In breaking free from the cycle, I discovered a profound truth. The rewards extended far beyond the physical transformation. As I shed the weight of guilt and shame, I found a newfound lightness of being. I experienced the joy of self-acceptance and the empowerment that came with knowing that I had the capacity to change my life. It wasn't just about losing weight; it was about gaining a life filled with renewed hope, self-belief, and an unwavering commitment to my own well-being.

As I ventured down this path, I discovered the transformative power of self-love, mindfulness, and forgiveness. These became the pillars upon which I built my new life. Self-love formed the foundation of my journey as I learned to treat myself with compassion, kindness, and acceptance. I realized that I deserved love, not only from others but from myself as well.

Mindfulness played a crucial role in my weight loss journey. By practicing present-moment awareness, I became attuned to my body's needs, recognized hunger and fullness cues, and made conscious choices about the food I consumed. Mindful eating became a way for me to nourish my body and soul, fostering a deeper connection to the food I ate and the impact it had on my well-being.

In the radiant glow of my newfound lifestyle, the Oumie and Zander Plan became more than a strategy; it was a tapestry woven with threads of hope, resilience, and transformation. Anchored by the perpetual melody of "Walking on Sunshine" by Katrina and the Waves, and the empowering resonance of my chosen power word, "brave," this journey transcended the ordinary and delved into the extraordinary. A magical metamorphosis occurred as these elements became interwoven into the very strands of my DNA.

At the core of this enchanting metamorphosis resides the extraordinary tool, Forever Song Anchoring—a key not merely unlocking the gates to each day but extending an invitation to dance in the realm of infinite possibilities. This isn't just a process; it's a beckoning to embrace the extraordinary within the ordinary, a magical alchemy that transforms each sunrise into a testament of potential for renewal and self-love. (If you're intrigued by the idea of infusing magic into your personal narrative of self-discovery and desire to transform your journey with the potent Forever Song Anchoring, explore my website.) Here, each note holds the promise of a brighter, more compassionate existence. Allow the melody to guide you toward a realm where hope reigns supreme and every step becomes a dance of resilience and grace.

But perhaps the most transformative aspect of my journey was the power of forgiveness. Its origins trace back to a pivotal moment during my second visit to the psychologist. His question echoed in the room: "Sanet, have you forgiven yourself?" In the silence of the car's parking lot, tears became the vessels for a cathartic release. Facing my reflection in the rearview mirror, I embarked on a poignant dialogue with myself—a conversation of forgiveness that spanned every mistake and every perceived failure.

The process was emotionally taxing—an hour oscillating between tears and words. Through this profound experience, I uncovered the transformative power of self-compassion and the necessity of unburdening myself from the weight of past mistakes. It was a crucial step, an act of self-liberation that propelled me forward, aligning my journey with the trajectory of the Oumie and Zander Plan.

Later that week, I wrote forgiveness letters to all the people who had wronged me, but the most liberating letter I penned was the one addressed to myself. In that letter, I confronted a truth I had long suppressed—the shame and guilt that had held me captive for not speaking up. I had carried the weight of that dark secret for years, always feeling as though an invisible sign on my forehead declared, "You can touch me anywhere you want!"

Releasing the burden of my silence was the most significant act of self-compassion I've ever undertaken. As a child, I had the mind and knowledge of a child, and the fear of potential blackmail loomed large over me. The Secret that held me captive was broken, and I set myself free from the chains of that painful past. It was an act of immense courage, and it marked a profound turning point in my journey toward healing, self-acceptance, and personal growth.

One of the stories I've told myself is, "Sanet never leave YOUR building!". Let me explain. My penthouse is situated on the top floor of this incredible, marble-adorned building that sparkles with elegance. I've even given my penthouse a name—Oumie and Zander Plan. As I ride the elevator (or lift in South Africa) toward it, something peculiar happens. When the elevator doors open on the second floor, I cautiously step out, my body still half inside the elevator. I look up and down, as if to question whether someone accidentally pressed the button. Then, the doors close, and the elevator continues its journey.

This peculiar moment in the elevator mirrors the times I've skipped a meal, didn't choose the right foods, or missed a workout. It's like a brief pause, a hesitation. But as quickly as I step out of the elevator on the second floor, I step back in, and it continues its ascent. These moments symbolize my determination to get back on track.

However, there are occasions when I'm lured by the alluring sounds and music on Floor 7. I disembark, visit 701, knock on their door, spend time there, and then proceed to 702, and so on. Each apartment visit represents a few days where I might not have eaten right or skipped exercise. But I've learned that I can't return to the way I was. I HAVE TO get back into the elevator, back on my journey to the Penthouse—the realization of my dream within the Oumie and Zander Plan to lose weight.

Floor 7 signifies the moments when I stumble in my fitness and nutrition goals, but my unwavering commitment to never returning to my previous self drives me to step back into the elevator and continue my journey upwards. I hope this mindful story inspires you to remain in 'Your Building' as well.

Inspired by my own journey, I created the Monarch Butterfly Programs, where I now share my knowledge and experiences to empower others who are desperately seeking change. Through these programs, I help individuals transform their mindsets and embark on their own journeys toward self-discovery and self-love. One of the powerful tools I utilize is my Facebook community, Diamond Beauties Forever, where an amazing tribe of women support and inspire one another. At the end of each day, I ask myself a simple yet profound question: "Sanet, did you leave your sparkle in someone's heart and memory today?" It reminds me of the impact I can make and the importance of spreading positivity and inspiration wherever I go.

By embracing these principles, I was able to lose weight, regain my health, and live a happier, more fulfilling life. And yes, my dreams came true. After three and a half years of not being able to see my beautiful family due to Covid-19, I finally had the opportunity to visit them in November 2022. I found myself on a swing next to my grandchildren, Zander and his new brother Zayden, laughing and enjoying each other's company. I love my life. I love my grandsons to the moon and back.

ABOUT THE AUTHOR

Sanet Van Breda Speaker/Author/Coach/Mentor. She is the founder of Self Love Ignites Me and Diamond Beauties Forever, as well as the newly launched Global Diamond Moments Magazine, currently spanning 35 countries. She is the driving force behind a heart-centered brand dedicated to promoting self-love, mindfulness, and personal transformation. As a certified Mindfulness Teacher, Master NLP Practitioner, Life, and Executive Business Coach, Sanet combines her expertise with her personal journey to create meaningful and impactful programs.

Her signature offering, the Monarch Butterfly Program, draws from her own experiences of weight loss and self-discovery, inspiring others to embark on their own transformative journeys.

Website: https://www.selflove4me.com
Website: https://www.soulofadimond.com
Email: slim@selflove4me.com

STACEY TUNTERI

Creating Space

Many of us have clutter getting in the way of our purpose in life. We have too many pairs of pants. Too many sets of dishes. Too many aspirational hobby accessories (ask me about the bowling ball and roller skates that sat in my basement for ten years). Too many toys, books, crafting supplies, etc. And that's just the physical stuff.

We also have mental clutter in the form of limiting thoughts and beliefs. A never-ending list of shoulds and shouldn'ts. Guilt. Regret. Imposter syndrome. Fear of failure. Fear of success! When we don't make time to clear out that head clutter, the gifts that make us unique and special end up dying on the vine, wasted.

Where does all the clutter come from? I can tell you how it started for me.

Throughout my education and career, my core identity was built on work ethic. It's an ethos based on hard work and sacrifice. We all absorb key messaging while growing up—a script that governs values and behaviors throughout life—unless we become aware of the script and take conscious action to rewrite it. The following is a list of the greatest hits from my early script about working hard.

- Life is a struggle.
- Opportunities are few and far between.

• Work is not meant to be enjoyed. It is a means to an end.
• You can't have and don't deserve a good life unless you work hard.
• If an employer has been good to you, you owe them loyalty.
• Women must work twice as hard as men for fewer resources and opportunities. Nobody said life was fair.

The prevailing themes are scarcity, fear, acquiescence, and subservience. According to my script, life is a zero-sum game. There are not enough resources to go around, so hold onto whatever you have like your life depends on it. Don't demand or expect more.

Accordingly, I said yes to nearly every job that was offered to me as a teen and young adult. Babysitting, food service, hospitality, landscaping, retail, office work, janitorial services, and gritty manual labor in a paper mill. The point is that my life experience taught me that hard work was essential for survival. If someone offered to pay me for work, I didn't ask what kind or whether I'd like it much. I just said yes.

Even after earning a master's degree, I took the first job offered to me, no questions asked. At a social services non-profit in Detroit, I connected folks recently released from prison with job readiness classes and basic resources. For nearly two years, I lived paycheck to paycheck, perilously close to needing public assistance myself. Eight years of overlapping odd jobs to get through school, followed by two years in my chosen field, had left me with a mountain of credit card debt, student loans, and a car that was always breaking down. I survived by clipping coupons and leaning on friends. I did not have a savings account and could not imagine a future that included one. It became clear that social work was not a sustainable career path.

From this nothing-to-lose place at age twenty-seven, I seized an opportunity to move to San Francisco and start over. When I drove my Toyota Matrix across the country, everything I owned in the world fit inside that tiny hatchback.

To kickstart my new life, I applied at a temp agency and took, yet again, the first job offered: administrative assistant. I remember sheepishly explaining to my mother, a lifelong secretary with no college degree, that after earning two advanced degrees, I would have the very same job as she did. But, because of the cost-of-living difference between Detroit and San Francisco, I was making more than twice as much money as an assistant than I had as a social worker. I was still helping people all day, but the stakes were comfortably low in comparison. Further, my colleagues were great, and I got to work in a high-rise with 360-degree views of the San Francisco Bay. As far as I was concerned, I had made it.

While I did demonstrate some financial responsibility by paying off my debts, I also went on wild spending sprees that make me cringe in retrospect. I discovered clothes in a major way. I bought purses, jackets, jewelry, and scarves. I bought shoes, shoes, and more shoes. As a quilter, I don't regret buying a nice sewing machine, but I have to scratch my head at the money I spent on sewing gadgets, accessories, and more yards of fabric than I could ever use in one lifetime. I also bought things for the house and enough office supplies to open my own stationery store.

Buying stuff was intoxicating. I couldn't stop. The dopamine hit of clicking the "Place Order" button in my online shopping cart kept me coming back for more. I filled closets and drawers, year after year until I ran out of places to cram things. Then I bought free-standing drawers, shelving units, and over-the-door shoe and bag organizers. Square footage in the house I share with my partner started disappearing, overtaken by all these mismatched storage solutions.

I continued working hard. I was promoted at work, taking on additional responsibility and earning more money. I worked at night and on weekends, going above and beyond my official scope of duties, because I was terrified of letting people down. Thoughts of unsolved problems, missed deadlines, or leaving someone hanging were powerful motivators that kept me pressing on at the office long after the heat and lights turned off. I would don a cardigan for warmth and wave my arms like those car dealership balloon men every ten minutes to keep the sensor lights on all night, to avoid disappointing people at work.

But I would disappoint friends and family at every turn because this was congruent with my script about hard work. I showed up late for dinner reservations with my partner and declined so many outings with friends that they stopped asking me to do things.

On my annual visits to see family in Michigan, I would bring my laptop with me. They thought it was crazy that I should be working while on vacation, but everyone in my family of origin had hourly jobs with clear start and stop times and compensation for overtime. I had no such guardrails in my salaried roles. I didn't know I was *allowed* to push back, much less how. Work ethic was my identity. If you raised expectations of me, I would stand on my tippy toes or get a fucking ladder to reach them.

Remember my early script about work? Don't leave a good-paying job with benefits because there may never be another one. If an employer has rewarded you with promotions and pay raises, don't get greedy by also asking for work-life balance. Besides, you're a woman, so suck it up. I ignored my discontent and buried my overwhelming dread of a wasted life in more clothes and shoes. I was always one mouse click away from the sweet relief of retail therapy, and I could afford it *because of this job*. I was a hamster on a wheel, going ever faster toward nothing.

Is your blood pressure going up as you read this? Mine is.

When my anxiety became manageable only by self-medicating and my marriage hit the skids, I saw potential ruin in my need to please. I had the stunning revelation that my particular brand of work ethic was, in fact, a lack of healthy boundaries. The scope creep and long hours were not my employer's fault. It was me. I had an unhealthy relationship with work, no sense of purpose, and I had developed an addiction to buying stuff to deal with it.

As they say, admitting you have a problem is the first step. Vowing to tackle one problem at a time, I started with clutter.

I made a pact with myself to not buy anything for a period of several months. Without the constant stream of new things coming into the house, I became more aware of what I already had. I started to notice what I rarely touched versus items I used often and with relish. I began warming to the idea of letting go of the untouched things. *This blouse is beautiful, but the fabric is chilly against my skin. I hate being cold. I am never going to wear it; the blouse can go.* This led to pleasant surprises like, *hey, I love this shirt! I didn't even know it was in here behind all this other stuff!*

I carved out a weekend on my calendar and decided to declutter an entire closet. It was so jam-packed that I nearly filled the bedroom with its contents when I started pulling things out, and it took me eight hours to clean out eight square feet. I was completely unaware that we possessed half of what I found in there. It was an enlightening experience. The following weekend, I tackled another closet. Then another, followed by an office clear-out where I blew out the motor on my shredder after emptying the fifth banker's box into it. The more I purged, the more irritated I felt about the sheer volume of stuff I had to go through, and the more ruthless I became when making decisions about what to toss or donate. Something unexpected happened. I started to get the same rush from putting things in the donation pile that I used to get when clicking the "Place Order" button!

In the midst of this process, we had the inside of our house painted. The project required us to box up everything we owned as though we were moving out and push all furniture to the center of the room, so the crew could tarp and mask before painting. When I realized how much stuff we had to pack, I got pissed. I purged aggressively before packing, and a month later I purged again when we put stuff away. Over and over again, I would say to various objects, "Why are you here? What value do you bring to my life?" Suddenly, it was easy to let go of my things, and the prospect of buying more stuff that I would later need to make these decisions about held zero charm.

Once I got off the hamster wheel of buying things, putting things away, or looking for stuff that was hidden behind other stuff, magic happened. I had free time. I was able to save enough money to leave my full-time job in 2019 and thoroughly examine my life. I got clear about what my values and boundaries are and began practicing techniques to help me honor them. I became conscious of the relentless stream of fear-based thoughts that kept me playing small. I also had enough time to finish decluttering the rest of my house. The spacious end result was better than any fix I ever got from shopping.

Finally, I asked myself the most important question. *If I could do anything I wanted for the sheer joy of it, what kind of work would I do?* In other words, what is my purpose? *THIS*. It really hit me then—the full impact that decluttering had had on my life. This process is not only about tidying up. It is an examination of one's life and desires and a resetting of priorities. It's an opportunity for empowering self-discovery.

This is what I do for others now. There is no better feeling than watching a client clasp hands to their chest and exclaim, "Oh, I had no idea I could feel this good in my own home!" They carry their good feelings into the world and shine their light on others. Facilitating transformation and creating space for what matters—*this* is my purpose. It is an honor and a privilege to work with clients who are ready to do this work.

ABOUT THE AUTHOR

Stacey grew up in the northern Upper Peninsula of Michigan. She was among the first generation in her family to complete higher education, earning a B.A. in Art and Psychology, and an M.A. in Community Counseling. After a life-altering event led Stacey to San Francisco, she pivoted from psychology to marketing administration in the California healthcare industry, but the calling to help people in a direct and tangible way never left her. After nearly two decades in healthcare, Stacey pivoted again, this time to professional organizing and coaching.

Stacey is a creative problem-solver, artist, writer, and efficiency enthusiast. She has deep experience in the transformative power of letting go of things, physical or otherwise, that interfere with living fully. She uses life lessons on patience, resilience, and staying curious to transform her clients's homes and lives.

Website: https://www.StaceyTunteri.com
LinkedIn: https://www.linkedin.com/in/staceytunteri

THERESE ALEMAN

My Life After My Husband's Death

You know that morbid joke—he was healthy, except for being dead? That was my husband. The person who meticulously attended every doctor's appointment, who had just been given a thumbs-up by both primary physician and cardiologist in the two weeks preceding, was setting up the grill when he dropped dead from sudden cardiac arrest on our lovely patio.

With something so momentous ready to catapult you on a journey you'd never choose to take, you'd think there would be a premonition, some sign. Yet, nothing on that sunny Sunday afternoon shouted, "Warning Therese Aleman, warning!" It was truly just a normal day. We had grocery-shopped and done yard work after completing an adoption for the dog rescue, where we both volunteered. We were preparing for a cookout with our children—a holiday celebration.

While he quickly lost consciousness and died, I stood in the kitchen, happily studying recipes for fruit salad. I went to check on his progress and found him. I searched for a pulse and put my head to his chest, trying to hear his heart beating, but didn't. I don't remember much after that other than grabbing my phone and screaming over and over, "Help us, help us, help us!"

I would discover weeks later that our video camera, placed there to record potential outside threats to our beautiful little life, instead bore witness to me running up and down the driveway barefoot and hysterical as I tried to make sense of what the 911 dispatcher was saying.

Neighbors rushed to do CPR while we waited for emergency medical attention. I was in a full-blown panic. Friends appeared to gather up our adopted and foster dogs and bring our human children from their jobs and Sunday afternoon activities. A couple, unknown to me before but hearing my cries from down the street, helped me gather my shoes and purse for a hateful trip to the hospital that I can hardly remember but will never forget. Another friend, my son and his fiancé appeared at the hospital just in time to hold me upright, as doctors said, "We did everything we could."

Later that night, support came from my two closest friends, who drove from another state to hold my shaking body, while grief poured out in palpable waves that reverberated around us. My best friend from childhood—my heart sister—says I kept repeating, "It was just a normal day, just a normal day," and that haunted her for months to come.

I was also about to learn the awful truth of widowhood that no one tells you—you die too.

Who I was—someone's wife, part of a team forged in the golden promise of till death do us part—the person I was for the better part of my adult life, was gone, just like that. His funeral was my funeral. The only me I remembered how to be right then died, just as surely as he did, and I grieved for her too, because there is no coming back from that. I wasn't going to rise from the ashes as my old self any more than he was, and I had no idea who I could, or even wanted, to be for the rest of my life.

Two years later, I have begun to build again. I'm still learning, but it's a complicated process. I hope what I have experienced so far brings a measure of peace to those coming behind me on this difficult road.

Let's start with advice for those of you who haven't even begun the journey yet. This is your opportunity to handle the business of dying *now* and to do these things while your brain is working normally, versus in a state of fog, shock, and incredible pain. There is a name for that: widow brain. It is real, and it can be crippling for the first several months, when you are least equipped to make serious, sometimes far-reaching decisions.

An example? My husband set up the account for our security cameras with a username and password, which, inexplicably, he didn't include on an otherwise expansive list of others. It was incredibly difficult to change the account to another email and password because, wait for it, it's risky to allow just anyone to change usernames and passwords on a security system. Of course, it is! Yet, it never occurred to me to think about that before.

So, Before You or Your Spouse Dies

Create a list of usernames and passwords for all accounts, including the obvious ones—banks, credit cards, insurance policies, utilities—and the not-so-obvious ones like the Wi-Fi, video surveillance systems, his/her and your emails, entertainment sites and online subscriptions, phone passwords, car entry keypads, etc. In most relationships, one or the other usually handles the business and financial aspects of the family. There's a 50% chance it's not you, so you may be left trying to figure out a litany of important things you didn't handle on a day-to-day basis, when you're grieving and just not thinking clearly. Make the list now—for both of you—and don't forget to include phone numbers and emails used for two-factor authentication.

Accept the Reality That You May Not Have a Warning

One of the hardest parts of my grieving and recovery was not having any warning that my husband was leaving me. I must have asked that question—why did you leave me? a thousand times in the first few months (as if he had control over it and chose the outcome that day). I had to process a lot of things when my brain and memory said, "We will not be reporting to work for a while"—survivor guilt, post-traumatic stress from events that day, the awful remorse that the last thing I said to him was a compliment on the grass looking healthy (as if I would have chosen those as my last words to the man I loved with my whole heart for more than 30 years), and those were just the mental and emotional issues.

I also struggled physically with anxiety, exhaustion, sleeplessness, sleeping all the time, not being able to eat at first, and using food as a comfort mechanism later. My blood pressure went up, my brainpower left the building, my weight went down and then up 30 pounds, and my memory got so bad, that I seriously wondered sometimes if I was starting to develop dementia on top of everything else.

What has this experience taught me? Live every day like you or your loved one is leaving because you just might be. Say the words, live the life, and accept that many emotions and physical responses are just going to be a part of your journey, no matter what. I've come to believe that sudden death is easier on the person leaving but harder on survivors in the first year, while illness is harder on the person leaving but the survivors have time to process. One of my happiest memories now is how my husband and I were holding hands and laughing as we walked through the grocery store. I remember saying, "I love you," after one of his dad jokes. I would have never even dreamed it would be the last time we'd hold hands, and say those crucial, life-affirming words.

No matter how we end up here, most widows struggle with anxiety, exhaustion, brain fog, memory loss, profound sadness, and then anger. My suggestion is that if you are in the early stages of widowhood, a trip to your primary physician can be helpful. I went to see mine three weeks in and ended up on the table, curled into a fetal position, crying helplessly and pouring out hurt all over her.

Now, I look back and know that even then, that was my first step on the road to healing. Over time, my doctor became one of my strongest advocates and helped me find other professionals I needed for healing and even growth as I became this new me that I didn't choose, but now accept and even like most of the time.

So many people, so little time

People say the darndest things. I learned this, and honestly, I've said some myself in the past, so I get it. I think most people want to help, but they have no idea what to say, so they open their mouths and inane platitudes fly out that, at the very least, don't help, and at worst, put you in a blind rage. "He's in a better place; you will find someone new; he wouldn't want you to be sad/worried/skinny/fat; how are you doing, accompanied by an uncomfortable look of pity, and call me if you need me."

People ask you for details of the death that you don't want to tell, quote scriptures that you don't want to hear, and offer help that never comes, and that's such a blessing! Really. I learned to rely on my tribe—a handful of people I could count on and truthfully tolerate in the days after my husband's death.

I know this begs the question: Well, then, what *do* you say? If it is someone you don't know well, saying I'm sorry for your loss is okay. If it's someone you do know well, tell them how much you appreciated their spouse, tell them you love them, or just do something kind and helpful. The things I appreciated most were gift cards for food delivery, people coming to walk the dogs, and my sweet neighbor mowing my grass

Another hard truth of death is that people are going to show you who they are, and when they do, believe them. It doesn't mean you can't have a relationship going forward—that's your choice, but you'll learn who your people are, and it is such a freeing experience! You *know* how precious time is. Why would you waste one minute of it with people who aren't a part of your tribe?

The Widowhood Recovery Timeline

There is no one-size-fits-all. We all process loss differently. I did learn a few things along the way that I think most of us experience, but your mileage on the road to recovery is going to vary, so please be patient with yourself and kind to yourself.

It took about six months for me to start thinking clearly again, but it came in spurts. There was no sudden lifting of the fog I found myself in. It just slowly dissipated. My memory slowly returned, but some details of that day and the days after, I still can't recover. I've come to accept this as my brain's way of protecting me.

We didn't inter my husband's ashes until about a year after his death. He was very clear that he wanted to be cremated, but never really talked about what he wanted to happen with his remains. Contrary to popular belief, there are going to be *many* things you won't really know about what your spouse would or wouldn't have wanted. The day we did inter his ashes was harder for me than the funeral, without that veil of shock surrounding me.

Year one also included all the holidays, the birthdays, and the anniversaries that marked our time together. They were brutal and I opted out of celebrating most of them. Year two, my adult children and I celebrated, but differently. Year three, we are settling into our new normal and I'm learning to trust myself, while honoring his legacy and our lives together.

Finally, there is no getting over this pain. You can only fall forward, but the bumps and bruises will lessen with time. I have learned to smile at memories, laugh at his quirky sense of humor, and that the heart has an amazing capacity to heal. I can only hope your journey brings you to this place of peace.

ABOUT THE AUTHOR

Therese is a journalist by training and a storyteller at heart, whether she's writing short stories, articles, journaling, or developing content for clients and companies. Therese was a pioneer in online marketing, learning search optimization and paid online advertising techniques from the ground up. She has also written content professionally for a variety of technology companies and as a marketing consultant and coach. Therese has a fierce love for her children and her German shepherds, all rescued dogs. She often shares her experiences on the journey of widowhood, life with big dogs, their rescue, adoption and training. A native Tennessean, Therese is a Vol for Life and a member of the Volunteer Club. She also enjoys writing about her faith and study of the Bible.

Facebook: https://www.facebook.com/theresealeman
Instagram: https://www.instagram.com/therese_aleman/

TRACY MANSOLILLO

Overcoming Adversity: The Road to Hope, Healing and Happiness

During the first 25 years of my life, I was truly blessed. I had a wonderful, supportive family and a childhood filled with love and happiness. I was given many opportunities to succeed, and I was hopeful about my life and the possibilities it offered. But during the next 25 years, I would not be so fortunate. That's when I experienced three major life disruptions that brought me to my knees and forced me to rethink everything in my life.

Despite having a strong foundation of life skills, unexpected challenges made me realize how quickly things could fall apart. Over time, my hope for the future would falter, leaving me with two choices. I could give up, or I could keep going.

Never one to shy away from a challenge, when life's first disruption hit, I wasn't initially concerned. I thought I had the flu, but after two weeks of high fevers, bone-crushing fatigue, and muscle weakness that made it difficult to get out of bed, I realized something was wrong.

I had no idea what lay ahead, but I was young and healthy. My doctor was puzzled by the ongoing symptoms and sent me to a specialist. The first specialist sent me to another one, and then another. During that first year, I visited many specialists as my condition worsened. I didn't understand why it was so difficult to pinpoint a cause and a treatment. Why was no one able to name or treat the mysterious illness that plagued me?

I tried to resume normal activities after the first two weeks. Each morning, I dragged myself out of bed, hoping I could make it through my workday. I'd return home and go straight to bed. On the weekends, I slept so I'd have enough energy for the coming week.

At work, walking up the flight of stairs to my office in the old mill building where I worked made me dizzy. Before lunch, I'd lay my head on my desk from exhaustion. Headaches, fevers, and muscle weakness continued daily. More concerning were the cognitive issues I noticed. I lost my train of thought while speaking with colleagues or had difficulty finding the word I wanted to use. As a marketing manager responsible for public relations and strategic communications activities, I was embarrassed at my inability to communicate simple thoughts. I struggled to do my job and worried about losing it. At the growing tech company, there was little room for error.

A few months passed. Still no answers. Doctors called it a post-viral illness and told me it would take time to regain my strength. When I began having issues with my liver and kidneys, my doctor forced me to take a temporary leave of absence. As sick as I was, I thought a few weeks of rest would be enough. Weeks turned into months.

When I saw a new doctor, I was questioned about the stress in my life as I traveled extensively and worked long hours. Many doctors wondered if I was just burnt out. Others suggested my symptoms weren't as bad as they seemed. They questioned my mental health.

I was ultimately dismissed because doctors didn't know better.

What followed were years of a mysterious illness that would ultimately force me to leave a job I loved, lose my livelihood, and question everything I believed.

I was 26 years old and too young to be sick. I sought answers and pushed to regain my life. It would take years before I was stable enough to resume working full-time. For a few years, I was able to manage my illness but flare-ups continued. When they hit, I used vacation time to rest and recover. I thought it was just how life would be.

I learned to accept not knowing what triggered my illness and committed to living fully despite my limitations. A few years passed without major setbacks, and I thought I was out of the woods. Then, adversity struck again.

I was married and had a beautiful son and two wonderful stepdaughters. I met my husband at work and later, we would start our own business. Life was busy. I was raising my son and building a business from the ground up. My health began to deteriorate again.

In my twenties, I had been diagnosed with chronic fatigue syndrome and told there was nothing that would help. In my late thirties, I was diagnosed with systemic lupus and treated at a leading hospital for several years. My symptoms worsened despite various treatments. During this time, I continued to question what was missing, even though my doctors didn't. Then even *they* began to question their lupus diagnosis, suggesting it could be another unknown autoimmune disease. At that point I stopped treatment. It wasn't helping. Rather, it was making me worse. I lost faith in the medical system. I decided to focus on being well instead of being ill. I thought I could magically wave a wand, change my way of thinking, and the physical symptoms would disappear.

I was wrong.

But soon, my health took a backseat when, without warning, my husband announced he was leaving. He had never seen me so sick, and it was clear the sick me was not the person he signed up for. Not only did he dismantle our family, but he took the business we had built and my faith and trust in others. A contentious divorce followed during which I would learn of his infidelity.

I spent years climbing my way back from a disabling illness and divorce. While I never stopped searching for ways to improve my health, it became less of a priority after the divorce. I was in survival mode. I prayed for the strength to move from one day to the next.

Slowly, with patience, faith, perseverance, and the love and support of my family, I regained my footing, built resilience along the way, and learned to find happiness and gratitude despite the many losses I had experienced. I began to savor the simple pleasures of life and enjoy every moment of being a mother. But the calm would not last long.

The bottom fell out of my world when my healthy 11-year-old son became ill virtually overnight. As I held his hand in the ambulance that sped to the local children's hospital, I wondered what I had done to deserve this latest challenge. Sitting in the hospital that night, I realized my illness and divorce were nothing compared to this. This was my only child. I was unprepared for what came next.

I watched my talented, three-sport athlete struggle to walk across a room without falling. A voracious reader, he now had difficulty following words across a page. My happy and confident child became reserved and resigned.

A new darkness cast a shadow on the light that had re-emerged in my life after so many years. I leaned on my faith and reflected on the past. I'd already experienced two life-altering challenges and survived. I reasoned if I could get through those, I could withstand this latest assault. But more importantly, my son needed hope and help. I forced myself to keep going and became a mom on a mission.

Thankfully, I had spent years studying psychology, metaphysics, and various forms of self-improvement. I had weathered years of illness, sadness, fear and uncertainty. I had built resilience and needed it more than ever. My journey through adversity was possible through a process I had developed over two decades, which included:

- Acceptance
- Perseverance
- Resilience
- Faith
- Mindfulness
- A growth mindset
- Self-love
- Self-awareness
- Support

I now believed I had the ability to overcome any adversity—the power to experience transformative change despite the circumstances. And if ever I needed to unleash that power, it was in June of 2017.

The doctors at the children's hospital did not diagnose my son's illness that evening. In fact, no one could determine what was happening to my child. I was soon thrust into a nightmare that wouldn't end. When local clinicians were unable to help we embarked on an 18-month journey through multiple states, traveling hundreds of miles to see dozens of specialists. But like a cruel joke, top doctors at the best children's hospitals could not tell me what was wrong with my son or how to help him. A three-day hospital stay in Boston resulted in more questions.

Determined to find answers, I began conducting research like a student cramming for final exams. After my son fell asleep each night, I went into my home office to read medical publications, journals and research articles. I followed every lead and talked to other patients and parents who were struggling to find answers. I reached out to clinicians around the country. I was desperate to find answers.

I scoured my son's medical records, creating a timeline and notes from every doctor's appointment since he was born. I filled large binders with test results, notes from appointments, and logs of symptoms. One night, I saw something that seemed to jump off the page. I hadn't considered at the time that when my son was seven, he had been treated for Lyme disease.

He had been playing baseball with some of the neighborhood kids after dinner one night. When he came inside, he told me his leg felt funny. There was nothing visible at the time, but early the next morning I found a classic bullseye rash near his ankle. I called his pediatrician and took him straight in. He said there was no need to do a Lyme test because the rash was a classic indication of Lyme. He prescribed two weeks of antibiotics.

It was June. Summer had begun, and my son seemed okay, but six weeks later, in early August, he developed a fever and flu-like symptoms. Every four to six weeks he would develop fevers, headaches, and joint pains. Each occurrence lasted a week or more. This cycle continued for years. His physician explained away each event, but I sought other opinions because something was definitely wrong.

Back in my office each night, I continued to compile my son's medical history, hoping it would help someone put the pieces together. My father, who was a physician, joined me in my search for answers. Soon, the timeline formed a graph, with peaks every few weeks marking his disturbing symptoms. The peaks started six weeks after the bullseye rash. I called the pediatrician to explain my findings and question whether Lyme could be the cause. He quickly responded, saying that my son was already treated for Lyme. When I questioned the persistence of the infection, he said it wasn't possible, yet I had read scientific evidence to the contrary.

I read every book I could get my hands on related to Lyme disease. And that's when I met an author and a parent of a child with Lyme whose story was so similar to my son's. She provided a lifeline when I needed it most. She recommended a neurologist in New York who specialized in Lyme and neuroinfectious diseases.

My son was too ill to travel, so first we had a telephonic consultation. The neurologist wasted no time ordering a battery of tests, including obscure blood tests that were done in labs and clinic all over the country, as well as an MRI. For the first time in 18 months, someone was taking his illness seriously!

We headed to New York when the results were ready. By this time, my son was in a wheelchair and had been unable to attend school for more than a year. We sat in her small, bright office, hoping for answers but not wanting to be disappointed. My son, who has a keen intuition and the ability to quickly read a room, would signal me within five minutes of meeting a new physician if they would help or not. He was right every time. This time, we didn't need to wait five minutes.

Looking directly at my son, with certainty and compassion, the young neurologist said, "I'm sorry for everything you have been through. I know what's wrong. You've tested positive for multiple tick-borne infections, including Lyme. We need to start treatment today. I know you'll have questions."

For the first time in nearly two years, I felt able to breathe. I couldn't stop the tears from falling. I was so relieved to have an answer and a caring clinician on our side. My son began treatment that same day and would continue for the next six years. He was later diagnosed with an autoimmune condition that was the result of inadequate Lyme treatment years earlier.

After the first trip, I returned home anxious to dig into the research and learn more about the complexity of his illness. I was disappointed to find a medical system that denied the existence of chronic, persistent, vector-borne infections despite physical evidence; an insurance system that refused to pay for treatment of chronic Lyme disease; controversy about how to treat Lyme; and questioning looks from anyone who asked how my son was doing. We continued traveling to New York every month for several years. We added other clinicians to his care team as needed; none were close to home.

Eighteen months after my son's diagnosis, during one of our trips to New York, I met with his neurologist and reviewed the results of tests she had suggested I undergo after learning of my illness. It was 2018, twenty-five years after first becoming ill, and I would finally learn the cause of my illness: Lyme and multiple vector-borne infections.

It was a cruel twist of fate. My son's illness and suffering had ultimately led to the answers I needed. But at what cost?

In time, I would learn more. I never recalled a tick bite or a rash at the time I became ill. Was it there but it had been missed? I needed answers. After focusing on my son's case for two years, I turned my attention to my medical history and compiled my records as I had done with his. Months after requesting my files, I was scanning the hundreds of pages, highlighting key test results, when I came across a positive Lyme test during the onset of my illness. It had never been disclosed.

Of course, I didn't receive treatment either, which meant I had a bacterial infection coursing through my body for twenty-five years. No wonder I had been so ill! When Lyme and other vector-borne diseases are left untreated, they can become chronic, persistent infections and lead to other more serious health conditions. I would also learn that Lyme can be transmitted from mother to child in utero.

Had I been properly and promptly diagnosed and treated for Lyme twenty-five years earlier, my son and I could have avoided years of severe illness and disabling symptoms, as well as hundreds of thousands of dollars in medical expenses, despite the best healthcare insurance available. Like millions of other Lyme patients, we had been dismissed and left on our own to find our way forward.

After denying the persistence of Lyme disease for decades, the CDC now admits that Lyme can become chronic and estimates there are 500,000 new cases of Lyme disease each year in the United States alone. Lyme experts believe the actual number of new cases in the U.S. is as high as 1–2 million every year. Because diagnostic testing is so poor, and the medical community is embattled in the 'Lyme Wars' millions of patients are suffering from chronic infections that have been left undiagnosed and untreated.

Patients are frequently diagnosed with chronic fatigue syndrome, fibromyalgia, multiple sclerosis, and various psychiatric illnesses, including depression. Misdiagnosis is rampant and patients are dismissed, delaying appropriate treatment and allowing the underlying infection to progress unchecked.

My story is not unique. It's one I've heard hundreds of times from patients and families whom I've met during my Lyme advocacy work. Lives destroyed. Families broken. A medical system ill-equipped to help the hardest cases.

What did I learn during these challenging times?

There have been many hidden blessings throughout my journey, but there's one that stands out. It's a gift to those who discover it:

It's easy to enjoy life's good times and joyous moments, the love of family and friends, and the successes one has achieved. It's far more difficult to find joy and happiness during the hard times, the darkest hours of life, when loss and uncertainty call each moment into question. If you can find hope and happiness during these times, you have everything you need to live a life of purpose.

Through adversity, I learned to cherish each day and live in the present moment with a grateful heart. Adversity taught me that vulnerability does not make you weak, and the past does not define you.

Adversity also led me to uncover my life's purpose: to help others with invisible chronic illnesses who have been dismissed and ignored. To raise awareness and funding for Lyme and vector-borne diseases. To give hope to others that even in the darkest times, there is light. To inspire others to build resilience and find answers.

My story may differ from yours, but no one is immune to adversity. When it strikes, I hope you know it's possible to overcome it. I hope you keep going, and never give up. We all have the power to transform our lives in meaningful ways, despite the circumstances we face.

I call it *The Power of Change.*

ABOUT THE AUTHOR

Tracy Mansolillo is a writer, mentor, advocate, and creator of ***The Power of Change.***

A former marketing executive, Tracy utilizes her unique combination of strategic planning and her experiences as a patient and parent of a patient dismissed by the medical system, to empower and help others.

When a life-altering illness struck her, and later her son, she was driven to find healing for them both. Tracy relied on her expert research skills and intuition, developing a roadmap that helped diagnose and treat her son, and solve a 25-year medical mystery. She shares lessons from those who stood by them, those who left, and those who helped along the way.

Tracy is the proud mother of a son who taught her what love means, a fierce advocate for the Lyme community and those with invisible illnesses, and passionate about helping others improve and change their lives by uncovering their hidden power.

The Power of Change on Substack: https://tracymansolillo.substack.com
Website: https://thepowerofchange.ck.page/home
Free Lyme Resources: https://tracymansolillo.substack.com/t/lyme-disease

YVONNE CÔTÉ

There Is An Angel For That

Color has always held a significant place in my life. From an early age, I perceived the world through a unique lens, where vibrant and enchanting colors would swirl around people, objects, and even buildings. Little did I know then that my perspective was different from the norm.

As a child, I was fascinated by the swirling colors enveloping people and things. When I shared this with friends, their reactions were far from understanding. Most would laugh or call me weird. Like many with unique experiences, I learned to keep this aspect hidden, which was a challenge as I realized not everyone saw the world as I did.

Growing up in an era without cell phones and the internet, I lacked the resources available today to explore or understand this phenomenon. Had I lived in the digital age, a simple Google search would have provided me with hours of reading on auras and their diverse interpretations.

After high school, entering the workforce highlighted the absence of my familiar friends. I felt I didn't belong anywhere, sensing insincerity in people's smiles and kind words. I questioned what I was doing wrong and what was wrong with me—I just felt like I didn't fit in anywhere. Eventually, I rationalized with myself, deciding to ease up on my efforts to blend in. It seemed that the more I reached out to people, the more I stood apart. In this phase, the lively extrovert of my childhood was fading, and by my early thirties, I had transformed into a complete introvert.

Life, at that point, seemed to be testing my resilience in all aspects. I had lost my job three times within the human resources sector of the pulp and paper industry due to economic downturns. It was a period marked by repeated setbacks and the sensation of starting anew each time. My professional life felt like a tumultuous rollercoaster ride, with uncertain job security adding to the complexities.

On the personal front, my journey was no less challenging. I had been married and divorced twice, navigating through the emotionally taxing terrain of separation and rebuilding my life from scratch, not once—but twice. These experiences, like the shifting tides of the sea, left me with a sense of constant chaos, and I yearned for stability and clarity in my life. It felt as though I was trapped in a loop of recurring patterns, marked by failed marriages and job losses, and feeling like I just didn't belong.

During this unpleasant period, I grappled with a pervasive sense of unworthiness that left me believing I wasn't deserving of love, a fulfilling job, financial stability, or meaningful friendships. The shadows of self-doubt and insecurity loomed large, and I felt hopelessly trapped in this cycle of negative self-perception.

It just felt like things were spiraling out of control. I was wishing that something could change—any kind of change, but now I know: be careful what you wish for. If you are not specific with

the universe, you just never know what you might get. The events that followed were completely unexpected.

I can recall browsing in a store one moment, only to awaken later in a hospital bed, disoriented and confused with a sore jaw. Once I recovered a little and became more coherent, I was informed that I'd suffered a severe head injury. My doctor conveyed that my being alive was a miracle since I'd absolutely been as near-to-death as he'd experienced in his career.

I tried to put together the pieces of what transpired. Remarkably, even to this day, I remain unable to recollect anything that occurred between the time of my injury and the moment I regained consciousness in the hospital, which was several hours later. Unbelievably, there was no pain in my head, considering the traumatic brain injury I'd experienced.

I spent a few days at home resting as per the doctor's recommendations, but I was anxious to head back to work and was determined to get my life back on track. The day I was returning to work started like any other day. I followed my normal morning routine and got myself ready for work despite feeling like I was in a bit of a fog. I got my kids ready for school, and off I went. Nothing really felt normal to me, and I couldn't explain why, but I chalked it up to just heading back to work after suffering a traumatic brain injury. My commute usually took me approximately 20 minutes since we lived in a rural area just outside of the city. What happened next was an absolute nightmare.

As soon as I pulled out of our driveway and started to drive, less than a minute later, I began to feel a weird sensation forming in the pit of my stomach. It almost felt like I was heading off to a job interview, and I was really starting to feel my stomach tighten, my heart race, and my anxiety level shoot through the roof.

The more I drove, the worse things got. My breathing started to become erratic, my jaw started to clench, and without initially realizing it, my hands were gripping the steering wheel so hard, they actually began to hurt. By the time I pulled into my parking spot, I was so nauseated that I was in a complete state of panic. I told myself that I just needed some fresh air and a glass of water and that I'd be just fine.

Except that I wasn't even slightly fine. What's even worse is that it didn't just go away after the first day. This level of anxiety accompanied me on every trip to the office that followed. The only saving grace was that I held a management position, and that meant I had the privacy of an office to myself. I quickly learned that alone in my office, I could manage some of the anxiety I was experiencing. A significant part of my job, however, involved actually speaking and interacting with people, so this made for some very intense and protracted days as I navigated my new reality.

This sensation of panic was on a whole new level. My alarm and anxiety eventually grew so intense that I became increasingly reluctant to leave my home and found it difficult to interact with anyone beyond my immediate family. Even the simplest tasks at work became more and more challenging to accomplish. I struggled to comprehend what was happening to me, and

despite undergoing numerous tests, my doctors were unable to identify any physical cause for my condition.

With growing dread, I came to the distinct realization that my job no longer aligned with my values. Something significant had shifted inside me; there'd been a cataclysmic change when I endured that injury to my brain, and I became acutely aware of the sense of disagreement I now held with many of the company's policies and procedures.

The toll on my health and well-being was becoming increasingly evident. I observed that whenever I needed to address my colleagues or discuss important matters around a boardroom table, I experienced a physical reaction; my voice would fail. It literally felt as though my throat was closing up, and I was unable to articulate my thoughts. Little did I know that one moment in the boardroom would be the catalyst for a complete upheaval of my entire life. The final penny dropped, and everything came crashing down.

As panic and anxiety began to tighten their grip on my life, I found myself increasingly trapped in a world of isolation. My social connections dwindled, and I felt a growing discord between myself and my children, who struggled to comprehend the invisible torment I was enduring. I could no longer attend all my kids' sporting events and school activities, missing precious moments that were once an integral part of our lives. The toll of my condition extended beyond my personal life; it reached into my professional world, rendering me unable to continue working. As the weight of my anxiety bore down on me, even my marriage began to show signs of strain, threatening the very foundation of my existence.

In the face of a challenging situation, my husband and I had to make some tough choices. We decided to sell our house, and even more remarkably, I chose to leave my job—a position I had worked hard for and dedicated a significant part of my life to. But the real shocker came when we made the decision to move 3,000 kilometers away to a place where we knew absolutely no one, leaving behind all the familiar support from my family.

This move, driven by my desire for a fresh start and the hope that a change of surroundings might bring solace, marked a profound turning point in my life. At the same time, my husband was dealing with severe burnout from his job, which required him to endure a grueling weekly journey spanning over 2,300 kilometers each way, combined with the demands of shift work and residing in camp conditions. The relentless pace was taking a toll on him, and we realized that relocating closer to his workplace was a necessity. Handling all the responsibilities and errands outside the home was piling up, adding to his burden. This move was our remaining hope of alleviating his travel-related challenges and fostering a healthier work-life balance. As for what would happen next, it was anyone's guess, but I was ready to take the leap and find out. I desperately need change.

At first, everything remained the same, and it seemed as though there wasn't much hope for improvement. As luck would have it, that didn't last long.

One day, in the midst of experiencing a bout of panic and anxiety, I became so distraught that I went to my room to lie down and find relief. I'm not sure why, but I grabbed the remote for the television. What I heard next was life-changing.

A woman detailed her experiences with panic and anxiety, and she too was unable to leave her house. Hearing someone else articulate so candidly about their struggles was such an overwhelming relief that tears leapt to my eyes.

The next revelation caught me completely off guard. She confided that she was a psychic medium, delving into her profound spiritual awakening, speaking of heightened energy, intuitive gifts, and a newfound connection to the spiritual realm. I was perplexed, confused, and intrigued all at the same time. How could someone who claimed to communicate with the dearly departed on the other side offer insight into my current situation?

Despite the persistent inner voice urging me to reach out, I hesitated, fearing judgment and skepticism. However, my desperation for answers and a desire for change overcame my reservations. I felt that continuing to live as I had been was no way to truly live.

Upon connecting with the woman, she received me with empathy. She listened attentively to all I'd been suffering, offering not only solace but also practical and profound advice to try. In the most unexpected turn of events, she became my first mentor.

Under her guidance, I embarked on a journey of daily rituals and practices that delved into the profound realm of spiritual self-care. Through her teachings, I gained invaluable insights into my true nature and a deeper understanding of the world around me. Energy, a central theme in her teachings, revealed itself as a force influencing us on various levels—emotionally, physically, mentally, and spiritually. This pivotal moment marked the initiation of my spiritual journey, a transformative path that would reshape my perceptions, beliefs, and ultimately, my life.

Shortly after I began my training, a vivid memory returned to me. I was sitting in the emergency room, and my doctor remarked that I must have an entire team of Angels watching over me, given how fortunate I was to have survived.

This is where I had an epiphany moment. All this time, I'd been searching for a medical reason or explanation for my panic and anxiety, and my doctors kept telling me there was nothing physically wrong. If there was no medical cure for me, could these same Angels perform another miracle and help me release the feelings of overwhelm and debilitating anxiety I was suffering from so I could take back control of my life again?

I was raised as a Roman Catholic, and of course Angels were mentioned in the church and throughout the teachings in the Bible, but my perception of them could be more related to the ones you would see around Valentine's Day— little cherubs who captured hearts for the sake of love. I had an image in my mind of this cherub-looking Angel, and honestly, I didn't really think much more about them. So, for the first time in a very long time, I had hope.

This moment sparked an incredible journey of angelic exploration for me. I dove thirstily into mastering the intricacies of these divine beings. I was hungry for every bit of information I

could devour. I literally could not stop learning about Angels. I became almost obsessed with them and amazed by the impact Angels could have on my life.

In the profound journey of my life, a pivotal moment unfolded when I recognized the vital role of spiritual self-care and the protection of my energy. This revelation marked the beginning of a gradual yet transformative process, leading me to reclaim my sense of self and reconnect with the vibrant, loving individual I once was. Through this evolution, I've cultivated the art of setting boundaries, embracing mindfulness, and surrounding myself with positivity, allowing my spiritual path to gracefully guide me towards a brighter, more balanced future.

I also learned that Angels can appear to you in colors. My heart overflowed with joy when I learned this because as a child, I could see colors form around people. I never understood what this was.

Colors have always played a significant role in my life, but I had no idea that they could have such a powerful impact, and I was inclined to apply the energy of color to my ongoing healing journey. Our chakra system is considered to be our life force energy, and each one relates to color.

During mediations, my Angels gently guided me in the direction of Reiki, and so began my next journey of healing and learning. This was an absolutely life-changing experience for me. Once I became a Reiki Master, I began practicing my own daily Reiki rituals, and was amazed by my own transformation.

As my personal journey of learning and healing reached its final chapter, I found myself irresistibly drawn to the mystical energies of the moon, the profound wisdom of numerology, and the transformative messages encoded within Angel numbers. It was as though the universe itself was calling out to me, inviting me to explore these cosmic avenues of understanding.

The moon, with its ever-changing phases, mirrored my own life's ebb and flow, teaching me to embrace each moment with grace and awareness. Numerology, on the other hand, unveiled the hidden layers of my existence, providing insight into my life's path and purpose.

Angel numbers, with their celestial guidance, illuminated the way forward, revealing the power of divine synchronicity. This final chapter in my journey symbolized a profound connection with the universe and its infinite wisdom.

Beyond my professional success, I've also found profound fulfillment in my personal life. I am in a deeply loving and harmonious marriage, where my partner and I share a beautiful journey of love, respect, and shared dreams. This relationship stands as a testament to the healing and transformation that have taken place within me, radiating love and positivity outward. It is a life that I had once thought was beyond reach, but with the power of spiritual healing, I have manifested a reality that has surpassed my wildest dreams.

Embarking on a journey of transformation and self-discovery was, for me, a life-altering experience. This journey was not just about me finding answers to the questions that were

weighing on my heart; it was about unearthing the innate power that resided within myself and realizing the profound impact it could have on my life.

By embracing the power of my intuition to follow my true life's purpose and by developing trust in my inner wisdom to guide me, I began a transformative journey. Additionally, as I learned to release limiting beliefs and heal ancestral wounds, I took significant steps toward realizing the life of my dreams. Through my exploration of working with Angels, tapping into the energy of colors, synchronizing with the moon's phases, and unraveling the secrets of numerology, I unlocked the keys to a life of limitless potential and boundless fulfillment.

You, too, can experience a profound shift in how you perceive and interact with the world around you. As you integrate these modalities into your life, you'll find that challenges become opportunities, uncertainty transforms into clarity, and despair gives way to hope. The power to manifest your dreams and create the life you desire is within your reach, and I am here to guide you on this remarkable journey.

My mission is to share the knowledge and insights that have brought light and transformation into my own life and to empower you to experience the same. By working together, we can tap into the extraordinary gifts that the Universe has to offer. Your life can be an incredible masterpiece of joy, abundance, and purpose, and it all begins with that first step toward transformation.

There are many Angels that can help in every area of life and in absolutely every possible situation. I have no doubt that whatever your situation is, There is an Angel for That, and if you're inclined to find out about how your Angels can help you, I'd be delighted to connect and discuss your unique situation. So, I invite you to reach out.

ABOUT THE AUTHOR

Yvonne Côté is a Holistic Wellbeing Practitioner, based in Kelowna, BC, Canada. Following a near-death experience, she felt called to work with Angels and has studied under renowned spiritual teachers and mentors to hone her talents. Yvonne holds multiple certifications as an Angel Practitioner and Guide, a Moonologist, a Numerologist, and a Color Intuitive. She's also a Reiki Master and a Crystal Healer.

Today, Yvonne specializes in empowering empathic women to break through the barriers of energetic blocks and to ignite their intuition through spiritual wisdom, unlocking their innate divine power, while embarking on a journey towards self-discovery and healing.

Yvonne also hosts the There is an Angel for That podcast where, she, along with her esteemed guests, discuss how to connect with your angels and offers tips on clearing energy and utilizing chakras to bring more balance to your life.

No matter what your situation, There IS an Angel for That!

Website: https://www.thereisanangelforthat.com
Facebook: https://www.facebook.com/yvonnecotethereisanangelforthat
Instagram: https://www.instagram.com/there_is_an_angel_for_that/

ABOUT SOUL PURPOSE PUBLISHING

SOUL PURPOSE
PUBLISHING

Founded by Dina Marais, the birth of Soul Purpose Publishing was inspired by Adriana Monique Alvarez of AMA Publishing. Ever since Dina read The Alchemist by Paulo Coelho, she dreamed of writing inspiring books like the author.

Taking the opportunity presented by Adriana took Dina's dream to a whole new level because as a publisher she could publish her own books and that of other authors. Dina believes that writing a solo book, or a chapter in a multi-author book, is like giving birth and the publisher fulfills the role of the midwife.

Dina chose the name Soul Purpose Publishing because it is her Soul's purpose to facilitate entrepreneurs to become successful through publishing their stories and coaching.

The vision of Soul Purpose Publishing is to give entrepreneurs a voice and make the dream of being published accessible and enjoying a personalized experience to become an Amazon Bestselling Author. Contrary to traditional publishing houses, the authors retain ownership, transparency, and control over their books.

The intention behind Soul Purpose Publishing is that through every book published, the author or authors involved contribute to the expansion of consciousness of all.

Contact Dina at publishing@dinamarais.com if you want to write a chapter in an upcoming multi-author book that resonates with you or to write and publish your solo book.

www.ingramcontent.com/pod-product-compliance
Lightning Source LLC
LaVergne TN
LVHW010653110826
845149LV00014B/3066